MW01172842

The One True Superhero

P.A. Strong

Winn Books LLC

PUBLISHED BY WINN BOOKS LLC – HAYDEN, IDAHO

Copyright © 2017, 2024 by P.A. Strong

Cover design by Mason Designs

ISBN: 979-8-9855016-5-0   *Printed in the United States of America*

Contents

If you enjoy this book, please leave
an honest review on Amazon.
Thank you!

1

The World Needs a
Real-Life Superhero

I t's the kind of stuff movies are made of—only it isn't a movie.

It started in March of 2020. A global health emergency was declared and people around the world were put on lockdown—*pandemic!*

Never in recorded history has there been such a coordinated global undertaking. Governments across the planet worked in lockstep to quickly restrict, mandate, and upend the lives of otherwise free people, leaving them isolated from society, and even their own families. Businesses were forced to shut down, creating massive unemployment that brought economies to near collapse.

Citizens on every continent were focused on one thing. Most stayed glued to their TVs for official updates and non-stop news, while death counts continuously crawled across the bottom of the screen. What started as panic quickly grew into a full fear-frenzy. Everyone was touched in one way or another.

They call it "the new normal"—like we need to get used to it. It's as if something snapped and everything around the planet has started to unravel. The 2020 spring lockdowns erupted into the summer of rage with uncontrolled riots; 2021 continued the grim news with political unrest, a major war in eastern Europe, and those relentless death counts; and many still aren't fully aware of how close 2022 brought us to nuclear confrontation or of the growing shortages of essentials, such as food and energy. Following this pattern of multi-front crises, 2023 didn't disappoint, with exploding turmoil in the Middle East that has escalated an unofficial WWIII to the brink. There's even talk of another pandemic. The planet rocks in crisis after crisis. Dare we ask what's next?

Now is when a real-life superhero would sure come in handy.

How are people dealing with such a dire outlook? Interestingly, most distract themselves with entertainment. One common attitude is, *Just focus on the positive.* All things considered, it's understandable. Why look at all that doom and gloom when you can escape into the digital world of make-believe? Since practically everyone has one, smart phones have become the standard distraction device.

Movies are a given when it comes to entertainment, and superhero movies are a cultural obsession. *The Avengers, Superman,* and *Spiderman* all have their own series, as does *Batman.* Each year there's another remake with a new twist on an old plot—someone with supernatural powers shows up at just the right time to deliver terrified citizens from their supernatural enemy and save them from destruction.

Superheroes come in all shapes and sizes. The overall plot is the various battles the villain wages against the hero, often turning his wrath on the innocent to provoke the defender of the defenseless. In the end, the hero always wins and the villain always loses; the world becomes safe once again, and everyone breathes a sigh of relief. Then the credits roll and the lights come on, and it's back to reality.

Reality is often a bitter pill. If 2020 was the poster child for bitter life, 2021 was the child turned troubled teen. And, yet, it's become so routine we barely notice the train of disturbing headlines anymore. The news is still full of disasters and heartbreaking stories of survival—and of those who didn't—and people we haven't elected have elected themselves to determine how these disasters play out. There is so much suffering today that we really need a super superhero!

For the average Joe or Jane, day-to-day life is rarely lived out on a global stage. We each have our own struggles that normally don't involve a pandemic or war. Every moment, someone somewhere is suffering—physically, mentally, emotionally, and even spiritually. Yet, our daily routine is sometimes so heavy that we just want to zone out for a while—which explains our smart phone addiction. It's a broken world full of broken people. We all know someone. We've all been that someone. Why?

This question can open a Pandora's box of other hard questions, and they deserve honest answers. Where do we find those answers? We won't find them by burying our heads in our phones and avoiding real life. Maybe the most obvious place for deep, honest answers is Almighty God. Wouldn't He have control over these things?

Those who deny belief in God are quick to point their finger there first: if God is real why does He allow sickness and violence and death? If I care enough to want to help, why doesn't He? Why does God allow such suffering when He has the power to stop it at any time? When answers don't come soon enough, it's sometimes easier to believe God doesn't exist.

The other end of the spectrum is only a little better. Those who do believe in Almighty God can't always explain these things either. Their personal consolation is that it is God's will and someday we will have all our questions answered, but for now we must trust in His supreme wisdom. Try telling that to someone in the midst of tragedy. Yes, even believers sometimes find themselves asking why it would be the will of a loving God for us to suffer.

There is a better answer!

In the eternal struggle of good versus evil, there is a real-life supervillain who is waging war against a real-life superhero, and this villain is using the human race as his personal pawn. But our superhero is truly a super Superhero who has more than enough power to deliver us from our enemies and save us from destruction, once and for all.

This is about the good news of Jesus Christ. He is the only, ever, honest-to-goodness, real-life Superhero.

To understand how the Hero saves the day, we must understand who Jesus really is and how His mission here on earth accomplished the most remarkable victory ever. We also need to understand the arch-enemy, Satan, aka the Devil, and why this ultimate villain has so much power to destroy.

Every good movie starts with a strong plot that the rest of the story is built upon. While some scenes are good enough to stand on their own, we can't fully appreciate the storyline and benefit from the message the author intended unless we see it as a whole, beginning to end. In the same way, we need to see the life of Jesus from beginning to end in order to fully appreciate it and benefit from the message God intended.

And if you've heard this story before, be patient and stay tuned. The plot has a whole new twist!

2

Backstory: A Brief Recap

W ho hasn't heard the story of the birth of Jesus, born in a stable, no crib for His bed? It's the stuff songs are made of. What else do you know about the historical Jesus?[1]

The Holy Bible makes a bold claim: Jesus Christ, the Messiah, is the only born Son of the only true God. That's what makes Him the only ever real-life Superhero! Jesus came to earth about 2,000 years ago on a life-and-death rescue mission to save the human race.[2]

While most of the world has heard about the birth of Jesus, not as many know about His life. As an adult, Jesus dedicated Himself to helping people and teaching them about

---

[1] Luke 2.

[2] *Messiah* is an Old Testament Hebrew title that means "The Anointed One"; *Christ* is the same title in the New Testament Greek. Luke 1:35; John 10:36.

God His Father. The jealous religious leaders rewarded His selfless ministry by plotting His murder by means of the Romans. But that wasn't the end for this Superhero; it was actually part of the plan. Because He had never committed even one wrong and didn't deserve death, God raised Him from the dead.[1] These historical events were foretold thousands of years in advance by Old Testament prophets and were later confirmed by eye-witness accounts.[2]

Yet, the boldest claim the Bible makes is that there is no other way, no other method, "no other name under heaven that has been given among men by which we must be saved" (Acts 4:10, 12)—not the name of Buddha, or Brahman, or Mary. No other name, but Jesus. Believe in and accept Jesus as the resurrected Lord of your life, and confess it to others, and "you will be saved" (Romans 10:9).

But, there's much more to the story. Jesus's mission was not only to heal the broken hearted and mend the physically wounded and handicapped. As a true Superhero, Jesus came to set free all who are oppressed by the arch-villain Satan.

> [18] *THE SPIRIT OF THE LORD IS UPON ME, BECAUSE HE ANOINTED ME TO PREACH THE GOSPEL TO THE POOR. HE HAS SENT ME TO PROCLAIM RELEASE TO THE CAPTIVES, AND RECOVERY OF SIGHT TO THE BLIND, TO SET FREE THOSE WHO ARE OPPRESSED,* [19] *TO PROCLAIM THE FAVORABLE YEAR OF THE LORD (Luke 4:18, 19).*

These caring acts of healing and deliverance fill in the storyline of a message to show the world how much God loves us. Still, there's more to the mission. In order for us to experience the reality of His Father's great love, Jesus came to save us from an enemy called Sin and its partner-in-crime, Eternal

---

[1] Thirty-one Bible verses state God the Father raised Jesus from the dead; He did not raise Himself: Acts 2:24, 30; 3:15; 5:30; 10:40; 13:30, 33, 34, 37, etc.
[2] Genesis 3:15; Isaiah 7:14; Micah 5:2; Hosea 11:1; Psalm 22:1, 6–18; Proverbs 8:22–31; Luke 1:2.

Death: He came to restore us to life. It's called the gospel, the "good news" of God's love for us as revealed through the life and death of His Son Jesus. Specifically, Jesus died for our sins, was buried in the tomb, and was raised up by His Father on the third day. Through this ultimate sacrifice on our behalf, God's unconditional love was on display.[1]

> *9 This is how God showed his love among us: He sent his one and only Son into the world that we might live through him. 10 This is love: not that we loved God, but that he loved us and sent his Son as an atoning sacrifice for our sins (1 John 4:9, 10 NIV).*

God loved us enough to make a way to save us, at His own expense. We're told that the power to save us is in the rightness of God, and the rightness of God is in the good news of Jesus Christ, and that faith is somehow the key to unlock it all.

> *16 For I am not ashamed of the gospel, for it is the power of God for salvation to everyone who believes (Romans 1:16).*

> *17 For in the Good News a righteousness [rightness] which comes from God is being revealed, depending on faith and tending to produce faith; as the Scripture has it, "The righteous man shall live by faith" (Romans 1:17 WNT).*

What amazing grace! Through the power of the gospel, we can be right with God. The only other option should cause us to shudder.

---

[1] Matthew 1:21, 23; 4:23; 9:35; John 1:18; 17:6, 26; 1 Corinthians 15:1–6.

¹⁰ This is how God's children and the devil's children become obvious. Whoever does not do what is right is not of God, especially the one who does not love his brother or sister (1 John 3:10 CSB).

Not having genuine rightness, or uprightness, means we do not belong to God and are not His children; rather, we belong to God's arch-adversary, the Devil. There's no middle ground. That makes it crucial that we know why we need the rightness of God, how to receive it, and what role Jesus has in it.[1]

¹ And you were dead in your trespasses and sins . . . ⁵ even when we were dead in our transgressions (Ephesians 2:1, 5).

⁹ All [are] under the power of sin. ¹⁰ As it is written: "There is no one righteous, not even one; ¹¹ there is no one who understands; there is no one who seeks God. ¹² All have turned away, they have together become worthless; there is no one who does good, not even one (Romans 3:9–12 NIV).

In other words, 1 Timothy 5:6 can apply to everyone: Those who live for their own pleasure are dead even while they live. So, without an intervention, we are the walking dead, destined to die permanently, because sin pays its wages in death—and we've all sinned.[2]

Facing death is pretty scary. But it wouldn't be as scary if we had hope that we could overcome the grave with a promise that we can live again when Jesus returns to this earth.[3]

---

[1] John 13:35; Psalm 24:5.
[2] Romans 6:23.
[3] 1 Thessalonians 4:13–18.

[24] Very truly I tell you, whoever hears my word and believes him who sent me has eternal life and will not be judged but has crossed over from death to life. [25] Very truly I tell you, a time is coming and has now come when the dead will hear the voice of the Son of God and those who hear will live (John 5:24, 25 NIV).

So, there really is hope, because we have a promise! But the scariest part would be if, in the end, we still had to face eternal death knowing we had been given an incredible opportunity to live again, an even better life, but we lost it by refusing to accept it.

[26] Then he will pray to God, and He will accept him, That he may see His face with joy, And He may restore His righteousness to man (Job 33:26).

To "restore" anything means it was once there, but was lost. When it comes to rightness, it makes sense that the rightness that Adam and Eve lost can be restored only from the original Source: the righteous God.

But first, we need to accept that God is not a theory; He is not some cosmic force or mystic energy. God is a real, living Person. Because He is God, He is the Source of all things, so He had to exist before everything. From the sheer vastness of the heavens to the most delicate fragrance, all creation testifies that God loves beauty and wondrous things; He loves joy and happiness. A creation full of wondrous beauty and joy testifies that He is a Person of deep feelings and emotions, though He is not driven by them as we are.[1]

[16] For God so loved the world, that He gave His only begotten Son, that whoever believes in Him shall not perish, but have eternal life (John 3:16).

---

[1] Genesis 1; Isaiah 45:5–8, 12, 21–24; 46:10.

God is often identified by His absolute love: "God is love" (1 John 4:16). Love is not just what He feels or does, but it is His very essence and nature—He just can't help Himself. It's one of His superpowers! On the contrary, our own nature is to love when it benefits us, so we humans have a hard time grasping the kind of love that God the Father has for us. What's more, He doesn't just love us, He wants us. He wants to have a personal relationship with us.

God loves and wants *you* so much that He was willing to sacrifice all of heaven for you. He proved that by giving His only beloved Son to ransom you from extinction and to restore you to what He originally created you to be. When God weighed your worth against the worth of His Son, He saw something in you worth the cost. And through His incredible Plan of Salvation, He made a way to have both you and His Son.

Once you experience another one of His superpowers—forgiveness—and can accept the truth of all that God has done for you through His Son Jesus, you will see yourself as He sees you, as a cherished member of His family; you will see your true worth and know your life has a deeper purpose. You will stop judging God based on how good or bad life is going for you, but rather on the profound sacrifice He was willing to make to restore you. You will find your true identity, not in the latest trend, but as a child of the Great King and your life will blossom into a beautiful, fulfilling experience.

> *8 And though you have not seen Him, you love Him, and though you do not see Him now, but believe in Him, you greatly rejoice with joy inexpressible and full of glory, 9 obtaining as the outcome of your faith, the salvation of your souls (1 Peter 1:8, 9).*

Don't forget that Jesus also loves and wants you, no matter how messed up you think you are. He knows every nook and cranny of your life and is not shocked or disappointed by anything you've been involved in. Jesus willingly went to the cross for you, so you can experience a better life—not a life of money and fame, but a more abundant life—the kind of life that fills all those empty places in your heart. See John 10:10.

Jesus accepts you just as you are. But make no mistake—He will never leave you the way He found you. He has superpower that can restore in you the rightness, or righteousness, that was lost.

But you may be astonished to learn what righteousness really is.

3
The Only Superhero with Ultimate Power

Righteousness is a big word in the Bible that many people have defined simply as "right doing." Unfortunately, the Bible compares all our righteous doings to a filthy garment. Even worse, whatever seems right to us will ultimately end in "the way of death" (Proverbs 16:25). Obviously, if we can't correctly tell right from wrong on our own, then our own definition of righteousness will not solve anything.[1]

> [16] For all that is in the world, the lust of the flesh and the lust of the eyes and the boastful pride of life, is not from the Father, but is from the world (1 John 2:16).

---

[1] Isaiah 64:6.

According to the Bible, every sin ever committed is rooted in one of these three causes: lust of the flesh (sexual, drugs/alcohol, appetite, etc.), lust of the eyes (coveting, greed, ungodly entertainment, etc.), or pride (self-promotion). Except for Jesus, everyone has been guilty of something.[1]

> [13] *Let no one say when he is tempted, "I am being tempted by God"; for God cannot be tempted by evil, and He Himself does not tempt anyone.* [14] *But each one is tempted when he is carried away and enticed by his own lust.* [15] *Then when lust has conceived, it gives birth to sin; and when sin is accomplished, it brings forth death (James 1:13–15).*

It would be normal to assume all we have to do is choose not to do these things and we'll be righteous—but that's human thinking. The truth may seem stranger than fiction. Righteousness is not what we do, or don't do. It's not a what at all, but a Whom. Indeed, all the good gifts of God are not things, but actually a Person. According to the Bible:

- Jesus Christ is our Righteousness
  (1 Corinthians 1:30; Jeremiah 23:6)
- Jesus Christ is our Sanctification (1 Corinthians 1:30)
- Jesus Christ is our Redemption (1 Corinthians 1:30)
- Jesus Christ is our Power (1 Corinthians 1:24)
- Jesus Christ is our Wisdom (1 Corinthians 1:24)
- Jesus Christ is our only Way to the Father (John 14:6)
- Jesus Christ is the Truth (John 14:6)
- Jesus Christ is the Life (John 11:25; Colossians 3:4)
- Jesus Christ is the Light (John 8:12; 9:5)
- Jesus Christ is the Word of God (John 1:1)
- Jesus Christ is our Peace (Ephesians 2:14)
- Jesus Christ is our Healing (Isaiah 53:5; Malachi 4:2 NKJV)

---

[1] Luke 4:1–13.

- Jesus Christ is the Door to the Father (John 10:7, 9)
- Jesus Christ is our living Bread of Life (John 6:48, 51)
- Jesus Christ is our Faith (Revelation 14:12 NKJV)

Another common belief is that the gifts and blessings of God come into existence as we ask for them. The sweet reality is that they are already available to us—and have been for the last 2,000 years! The reason the Son of God became the Son of Man was to become everything we need but couldn't provide for ourselves—the basic definition of a superhero. Every blessing we'll ever need has been available to us ever since God's Son completed His mission on earth. God does not need to create a remedy for each problem we face. Our remedy today is the same Remedy as it was in the days of the apostles.

For example, Jesus said, "Abide in Me, and I in you. As the branch cannot bear fruit of itself unless it abides in the vine, so neither can you unless you abide in Me" (John 15:4). Think about this logically. A branch doesn't struggle to produce fruit through willpower. The fruit comes naturally because of the vine it grows from: A good vine produces good fruit; a bad vine produces bad fruit. If we have a healthy connection to Jesus, we will naturally produce Jesus-fruit. In simple terms, good works are not the root, but the fruit of a relationship with Jesus.

So, if Jesus actually abides in us, and we in Him, then as long as we continue to abide in Him we have eternal life already, because He has eternal life in Him. Likewise, if Jesus is our peace, then abiding in Christ will give us peace instead of bitterness and anger, and we won't find ourselves ranting against those who fail us or depressed when life takes a sour turn.

Again, Jesus is the Truth, so our search for truth isn't for the right set of doctrines, but for Jesus Himself. But don't worry—He will lead us into true doctrine because what we believe about God and His Son determines the strength of our faith in and relationship with Them. The reverse is also true: A false belief of God and His Son will weaken our faith in and relationship with Them. "Whatever is not from faith is sin" (Romans 14:23).

Do we need healing? Jesus is the remedy for that too. We don't need to ask if it is God's will for healing. God has already provided the healing in His Son, because with His stripes we "were healed" (1 Peter 2:24). Instead of seeking healing, then, we need to seek Jesus; seek to know Him better until His life becomes our life, until His faith becomes our faith, until we have "the faith of Jesus" (Revelation 14:12 NKJV). Seek Jesus and every blessing we need will fall into place—He is the blessing!

Let's be clear though. Seeking Jesus is not about what we can get out of Him. It's not like Gotham City sending a signal to Batman only to come when there's trouble. It is all about friendship.

*19 And my God will supply all your needs according to His riches in glory **in** Christ Jesus (Philippians 4:19).*

It follows that if Christ is our Righteousness, then righteousness is not "right doing" after all. It is living and abiding in Him, because wherever Jesus is there is righteousness. This should clear up what our part is in God's plan to save us. We don't work toward anything except abiding in Jesus by fighting "the good fight of faith" (1 Timothy 6:12). Then Christ will work righteousness in us, which is exactly what we're promised.

*13 For it is God who is at work **in** you, both to will and to work for His good pleasure (Philippians 2:13).*

[21] *Equip you in every good thing to do His will, working **in** us that which is pleasing in His sight, **through** Jesus Christ, to whom be the glory forever and ever. Amen (Hebrews 13:21).*

God works through Jesus to give us even the desire to do His good pleasure. However, when we believe righteousness is what we do, our focus shifts from Jesus, who is our Righteousness, to our self, who must produce righteousness—and we can't produce or create any good thing. This fixation on behavior and whether we're obeying all the rules leads us to believe our problem with sin is because we're not choosing to do right and, instead, choosing to do wrong. Since by beholding we become changed, we become whatever we are fixated on—more wrong-doing. Our relationship with God becomes overshadowed by our focus with sin versus the law and, whether we think so or not, we end up believing salvation is by obeying the law.[1]

With this mindset, we tend to believe that we can fall in and out of salvation based upon how we behave. Because of our faulty viewpoint, we start to see God through our own eyes, as a stern judge ready to smite us if we mess up. We judge Him as being fixated on enforcing justice because His law was broken. This is legalism.

First, we need to recognize that God is not mad at us when we mess up. He loves us and knows our limits without Him. Second, we need to recognize that our real problem is not breaking the law, therefore, keeping the law is not our answer. Behavior is a fruit of the nature we possess. We believe we need to change our behavior when what we need is a new nature, to become attached to a new vine, to actually get a new life. Our doings, our works, our acts of sin, are only symptoms of what's inside.[2] Jesus said:

---

[1] 2 Corinthians 3:18.
[2] Proverbs 23:7; Galatians 2:16.

²⁰ That which proceeds out of the man, that is what de-filed the man. ²¹ For from within, out of the heart of men, proceed the evil thoughts, fornications, thefts, murders, adulteries, ²² deeds of coveting and wickedness, as well as deceit, sensuality, envy, slander, pride and foolish-ness. ²³ All these evil things proceed from within and de-file the man (Mark 7:20–23).

⁴⁵ The good man out of the good treasure of his heart brings forth what is good; and the evil man out of the evil treasure brings forth what is evil; for his mouth speaks from that which fills his heart (Luke 6:45).

The actions of the sins of the flesh begin in the heart. Again, true righteousness is not doing anything; it is a Person —Jesus Christ. The lack of righteousness is the lack Jesus's presence.

4
The Major Principle
of the Universe

The number one universal truth all others are based upon is that there is only one God.[1]

4 Hear, O Israel! The LORD is our God, the LORD is one! (Deuteronomy 6:4).

6 Yet for us there is but one God, the Father, from whom are all things and we exist for Him; and one Lord, Jesus Christ, by whom are all things, and we exist through Him. 7 However not all men have this knowledge (1 Corinthians 8:6, 7).

---

[1] Romans 3:30; 1 Corinthians 8:4.

*⁴ There is one body and **one Spirit,** just as also you were called in one hope of your calling; ⁵ **one Lord,** one faith, one baptism, ⁶ **one God and Father** of all who is over all and through all and in all (Ephesians 4:4–6).*

The Bible calls the Father the one God and Jesus the one Lord, the Son of the one God.[1]

¹⁸ And Jesus said to him, "Why do you call Me good? No one is good except God alone" (Mark 10:18).

The major *principle* working in the universe is the fact that God alone is good. It is His divine nature. God is good; therefore, true good is God. It's another one of His superpowers. Separate from God and the Source for goodness is gone. What is left is pure evil, a heart that lacks any goodness. This is sin.

Before the fall, Adam and his Creator were in perfect harmony because Adam was made in God's image. When Adam rebelled against God, it created a division, or divorce, in their relationship. This estrangement from the good God resulted in a sin nature (carnal nature/spirit) in Adam. What followed was sinful behavior.

Using the basic rules of grammar, think of it as the difference between a state of being (noun) and an action (verb). It's the state of being that produces the action. In other words, actions are evidence of the nature they flow from, just as the type of fruit is evidence of the kind of vine it's growing on. In this case, it's the nature of sin that produces the acts of sin. Correct only the acts of sin and the root of the sin nature is still alive and healthy. Despite the greatest efforts, eventually it will produce what comes naturally—more sinful acts.

---

[1] More details on this later.

Paul, who had persecuted believers in the name of God (see Galatians 1:13), explained his life before Jesus:

*¹⁴ We know that the law is spiritual; but I am unspiritual [carnal], sold as a slave to sin. ¹⁵ I do not understand what I do. For what I want to do I do not do, but what I hate I do. ¹⁶ And if I do what I do not want to do, I agree that the law is good. ¹⁷ As it is, it is no longer I myself who do it, but it is **sin living in me.** ¹⁸ For I know that good itself does not dwell in me, that is, in **my sinful nature.** For I have the desire to do what is good, but I cannot carry it out. ¹⁹ For I do not do the good I want to do, but the evil I do not want to do—this I keep on doing. ²⁰ Now if I do what I do not want to do, it is no longer I who do it, but it is **sin living in me that does it.** ²¹ So I find this **law** at work: Although I want to do good, evil is right there with me. ²² For in my inner being I delight in God's law; ²³ but I see another law at work in me, waging war against the law of my mind and making me a prisoner of **the law of sin at work within me.** ²⁴ What a wretched man I am! Who will rescue me from this body that is subject to death? (Romans 7:14–24 NIV).*

This long passage is important. Paul described an entity called *sin* living inside him. This slave-master, *this law,* warred against his mind and enslaved him to the law of sin in his body. This is not a legal law, so it is not a behavior issue. It's a law of nature, a natural law, a result of Adam's fall. It prevented Paul from doing the good that he desired and demonstrates the power of the nature of sin.

When Adam chose the lies that Satan spun in the Garden of Eden, that choice had a far-reaching impact: It sold us all under *sin,* a villain so strong that we cannot overpower it on our own. We are captives, at its mercy. Then while in this broken state, we must contend with the real Dark Lord himself![1]

In case you missed it, humanity's problem is not what we do, but who we are. We are carnal *by nature,* in our very essence. Thus, what comes out of us is carnal at the root and is against the will of God. We may not even realize the depth of depravity that we are capable of because we have always had the holy Spirit acting on our consciences.

> [9] *The heart is more deceitful than all else and is desperately sick; Who can understand it? (Jeremiah 17:9).*

Immediately after the fall of Adam and Eve God introduced a plan to redeem them and their future family from the choice they had just made. This urgent response to that crisis has shielded us from experiencing the full extent of what the carnal heart is capable of, though at times, as throughout history, we see it at work in all its ruthless cruelty. The spirit of rebellion that we witness in openly evil people would be thriving in us as well, without the intervention of the Spirit of Christ continually drawing us, convicting us, even when we don't realize it.[2]

Still, we fool ourselves into believing we can choose our way out of sin. The apostle Paul's choice was to keep the law, but he couldn't. Neither can we; it's a fight against nature. Our willpower can take us only so far before we fail. Miserably. Again. We cannot change who we are any more than rain can choose to fall upward—the laws of nature prevent it. So, what chance do we have? Where do we find help?

> [10] *He has not dealt with us according to our sins, nor rewarded us according to our iniquities (Psalm 103:10).*

---

[1] Genesis 3:1–7.
[2] John 12:32; 6:44; 16:8; Acts 3:26.

Thankfully, God is love. In that love, He is merciful and doesn't judge us in our weaknesses. Even if your past is dark, with sins and mistakes you dare not repeat to others, you don't have to carry that baggage of guilt forever. Do not let the Evil Overlord convince you that you've done too much for God to forgive. Do not believe that God is against you. Your Father is calling you. It's never too late.

> *[11] For as high as the heavens are above the earth, so great is His lovingkindness toward those who fear Him. [12] As far as the east is from the west, so far has He removed our transgressions from us. [13] Just as a father has compassion on his children, so the LORD has compassion on those who fear Him. [14] For He Himself knows our frame; He is mindful that we are but dust (Psalm 103:11–14).*

The fact that your mistakes bother you shows He is still working on your heart. So, don't worry that you're not good enough. God has deep compassion for you because He knows you are but dust and that apart from Him you "can do nothing" (John 15:5). God is the One who has placed in your heart a yearning for more than this present life by giving you "a measure of faith" (Romans 12:3). You can trust He hasn't left you to struggle on your own against such a mighty Adversary. It was in this very state of emergency that Jesus stepped in to save the day![1]

> *[6] For while we were still helpless, at the right time Christ died for the ungodly. [7] For one will hardly die for a righteous man; though perhaps for the good man someone would dare even to die. [8] But God demonstrates His own love toward us, in that while we were*

---

[1] 2 Corinthians 7:10; Isaiah 55:7; Psalm 41:2.

yet sinners, Christ died for us (Romans 5:6–8).

[10] For . . . while we were enemies we were reconciled to God through the death of His Son (Romans 5:10).

How did God prove His unconditional love for you? By sending His very Son to challenge and conquer your worst enemy—*when you were that enemy.* Like Paul, though, you have the answer to your dilemma: "Thank God! The answer is in Jesus Christ our Lord" (Romans 7:25 NLT).

What freedom to know that God never intended for any of us to choose our way out of sin!

When the one true Superhero came to earth, He took on the form of a simple human. By learning about Jesus's position as the last Adam, it may help us see how we can overcome the wrong choice of the first Adam.

5

The Two Adams and the Law of Inheritance

When God created man, He created only one life, and that one life was Adam. Every life after that came from Adam. Even Eve was an extension of Adam's life.[1] Since then, every time a child is born, God doesn't recreate life. Instead, life comes by inheritance from Adam through biological reproduction.[2]

God built the law of heredity into all creation; every living thing reproduces "after his kind." See Genesis 1:11 KJV, etc. That's why we don't worry that our precious baby will be born

---

[1] Creation of the world occurred about 6,000 years ago, not billions. For extensive scientific evidence for a recent creation and man's origins, visit https://answersingenesis.org/. Disclaimer: *TMOTG* does not endorse everything Answers presents, scientifically or spiritually.
[2] Genesis 2:7, 21–23; 1 Corinthians 11:8.

a baboon. We are humans by nature because we've inherited Adam's human nature. This is a law of nature.[1]

> [16] *The highest heavens belong to the LORD, but the earth he has given to mankind (Psalm 115:16).*

God created Adam to be the official representative and head of planet earth and instructed him to "subdue it" and "have dominion" over everything in it. See Genesis 1:28 KJV. This implies there would not have been disease, blight, and natural disasters, etc., before sin because Adam, in harmony with God, would not have allowed it. Every created thing, including man, was "very good." (Genesis 1:31) It was paradise!

> [12] *Therefore . . . through one man sin entered into the world, and death through sin, and so death spread to all men, because all sinned (Romans 5:12).*

Adam was created with free will—the power of choice. Sadly, Satan manipulated Adam and Eve into accepting his lies about their Creator. As father of the human race, what Adam chose in the Garden of Eden he chose for everyone, before anyone was even born. Adam's great sin was that he chose to separate from God, the only Source of life and goodness. And because everything produces after his kind, when Adam's nature became corrupted, the whole stream of humanity became corrupted. We're still humans (physically), but we're no longer righteous (spiritually) as Adam was before he sinned. This is our inheritance.[2]

By enticing just one man to separate from God, Satan usurped the dominion that God had given to Adam, which

---

[1] Example: cats (felines), whether big or small, have always produced baby cats, and only baby cats.

[2] Genesis 3:1–13; 5:3. We each have individual identity, and we also have a corporate identity as members of a group called the human race, descendants of one man and one woman.

brought a curse on the once-perfect planet. In a way, we are all victims of Adam's choice.

> *⁶ For to be carnally minded is death, but to be spiritually minded is life and peace. ⁷ Because the carnal mind is enmity [hostile] against God; for it is not subject to the law of God, nor indeed can be. ⁸ So then, those who are in the flesh cannot please God (Romans 8:6–8 NKJV).*

The result was permanent. Once Adam's mind became separated from God, he had no ability on his own to turn back. Remember, only God is good; therefore, Adam could not make the good choice for God without God. Thus, mankind became a carnal race and God's chief rival took command of Planet Earth.[1]

God knew the man and his wife had fallen. Yet, as usual, He came to visit His friends that evening. Were Adam and Eve happy that God came calling? No, they hid from Him! This shows man's sin did not estrange God from man but man from God. Immediately, he became at enmity with his Maker and avoided Him. Their relationship was shattered because Adam now felt hostility towards his Creator! Then when questioned about their odd behavior, the couple's first instinct was to point fingers: Adam blamed Eve and Eve blamed the serpent. It may well have been their first fight.[2]

The importance of this cannot be overlooked. Due to the *natural law of consequences,* every child is born in the likeness of his father Adam, in his carnal spirit and at enmity with God by nature. This nature is self-preserving, self-destructive, and programmed to sin. The carnal heart is intent on living independent of the Creator, so in reality it is destined for death because it is cut off from the only Source of life. It is

---

[1] Romans 1:28–31; Luke 4:5, 6; John 12:31; 14:30; 16:11; 2 Corinthians 4:4; Ephesians 2:2.
[2] Genesis 3:8–10.

only God's abundant grace that is keeping us alive!

Because it is impossible for carnal beings to change their mind and go back to God in their own power, they can never return to their original purpose of love and be at peace with God. They can never live a holy life. They can never live, period. Determining to "do right" is only superficial and temporary at best because the law of nature overpowers personal choice.

Real, permanent change can come only by changing our *nature*—who we are in our innermost being. This cannot happen naturally. Our only hope is for something *super*natural—a miracle. Thankfully, the story does not end here. This is where our real-life Superhero comes to save the day—and He specializes in miracles!

> *²¹ So that, as sin reigned in death, even so grace would reign through righteousness to eternal life through Jesus Christ our Lord (Romans 5:21).*

The law of inheritance is true both physically and spiritually. As the first Adam is the source of our physical life and nature, so the last Adam, Jesus Christ, is the Source of our eternal life and spiritual nature.

> ⁴⁵ *So also it is written, "The first **man,** Adam, **became a living soul."** The last Adam [Jesus] became a life-giving spirit (1 Corinthians 15:45).*

Since the sin nature is a state of being, it is naturally carnal, regardless of any sinful behavior and independent of the guilt resulting from such behavior. This means that before we even committed an act of sin we were already at enmity with God by our very existence. This is not to be confused with the concept of "original sin" which teaches the *guilt* of Adam's sin was passed down to his children, not his fallen nature. While we are all born with a sin nature, we become guilty only after we've knowingly committed a wrongful act.[1]

In a courtroom, a person is pronounced guilty not because he was born on the wrong side of the tracks (inherent), but because he has been determined to have committed a crime. Thus, while the sin nature produces sin behavior, it is sinful behavior which produces guilt.

Frankly, we were just born wrong the first time. That is why Jesus said we must be *born again*. Being born again starts with recognizing your need for a Savior and repenting, that is, turning your back on your old life of the flesh toward something better. That "something better" is Jesus. He does the rest.

> [5] *Jesus answered, "Truly, truly, I say to you, unless one is born of water and the Spirit he cannot enter into the kingdom of God.* [6] *That which is born of the flesh is flesh, and that which is born of the Spirit is spirit.* [7] *Do not be amazed that I said to you,* **You must be born again** *(John 3:5–7).*

> [19] *Repent therefore and be converted [born again], that your sins may be blotted out, so that times of refreshing may come from the presence of the Lord (Acts 3:19 NKJV).*

> [19] *For as through the one man's [Adam's] disobedience the many were made sinners, even so through the obedience of the One [Christ] the many will be made righteous (Romans 5:19).*

Jesus Christ is the Father of a new race of born-again children. As the last Adam, Jesus also produces life after His kind through inheritance. In the *new birth* experience, our carnal

---

[1] See Ezekiel 18:20.

nature—not our physical bodies—inherited from the first Adam, died when Christ died and was buried with Him in the tomb. When He was resurrected, we were resurrected with Him into a new life. This reality becomes ours the moment we accept Him.

> *³ Or do you not know that all of us who have been baptized into Christ Jesus have been baptized into His death? ⁴ Therefore we have been buried with Him through baptism into death, so that as Christ was raised from the dead through the glory of the Father, so we too might walk in newness of life. ⁵ For if we have become united with Him in the likeness of His death, certainly we shall also be in the likeness of His resurrection (Romans 6:3–5).*

Jesus doesn't fix our fallen nature, and that's because we're not fixable. He recreates us totally new!

> *⁶ Knowing this, that our old self was crucified with Him, in order that our body of sin might be done away with, so that we would no longer be slaves to sin; ⁷ for he who has died is freed from sin. ⁸ Now if we have died with Christ, we believe that we shall also live with Him (Romans 6:6–8).*

So, clearly, it is not by anything we do, or even can do. *We* cannot put our own carnal nature to death and resurrect ourselves into something entirely new and pure: It's not spiritual suicide. Rather, it's spiritual crucifixion with Jesus. And it's all according to the remarkable power of this remarkable, miracle-working Savior.[1]

---

[1] 2 Corinthians 4:6, 7.

*[17] Therefore, if anyone is **in** Christ, he is a new creation; old things have passed away; behold, all things have become new (2 Corinthians 5:17 NKJV).*

*[3] Blessed be the God and Father of our Lord Jesus Christ, who according to His great mercy has caused us to be **born again** to a living hope through the resurrection of Jesus Christ from the dead (1 Peter 1:3).*

In the miracle of new birth, we *put on* Christ Jesus, and by so doing, our old desires are reversed: His thoughts become our thoughts, His desires become our desires, His righteousness becomes our righteousness in such a way that we are "made the righteousness of God *in* Him" (2 Corinthians 5:21 KJV). This is His own righteousness restored in us!

*[14] But **put on** the Lord Jesus Christ, and make no provision for the flesh in regard to its lusts (Romans 13:14).*

*[23] And be renewed in the spirit of your mind; [24] and that you **put on** the new man [Christ Jesus] which was created according to God, in true righteousness and holiness (Ephesians 4:23, 24 NKJV).*

Putting on Jesus is the same as abiding in Him. The reason we put Him on is because He is the Armor that we are to be covered in: the belt of Truth, the breastplate of *Righteousness,* the shoes of *Peace,* the shield of *Faith,* the helmet of *Salvation,* and the Sword of the *Spirit,* which is *Word* of God. See Ephesians 6:10–18. Jesus is the ultimate Superpower!

[10] If Christ is in you, though the body is dead because of sin, yet the spirit is alive because of righteousness (Romans 8:10).

At the same time you are made new, you are also made dead to sin because your old carnal self has died, crucified with Christ on the cross. This reality happens spiritually, *by faith,* by believing it is so because God said it is so—without questioning how—because "it is impossible for God to lie" (Hebrews 6:18).

Being born again, you are now re-created to perform the good works that please God.

> *[8] For by grace you have been saved through **faith;** and that not of yourselves, it is the gift of God; [9] not as a result of works, so that no one may boast. [10] For we are His workmanship, created **in** Christ Jesus for good works, which God prepared beforehand so that we would walk in them (Ephesians 2:8–10).*

Our own faith is intellectual, in the mind. We may see evidence for believing, but it has no power to transform us—even demons believe in God and His Son. Sometimes faith is little more than emotion, like those who followed Christ for the miracles, but not for *Him.* True faith, however, in the spirit, is a gift from God. This is the faith that believes unto salvation—and can move mountains.[1]

Grace is defined as *"the divine influence [of the Spirit] upon the heart and its reflection in the life"* (Strong's Concordance, G5463). Grace is Jesus being willing to use His divine superpower to fill you with the kind of faith that allows Him to then change you into His perfect image. Everything is from and through Him!

---

[1] James 2:19; Luke 4:33; John 2:23, 24; Philippians 1:29.

6

The Superhero Who Joined the Human Race

It's vital we understand that Jesus did not die on the cross at Calvary as punishment to pay a *legal* penalty for us breaking the law. That is, the Sovereign God of the universe did not sacrifice His only Son in our place in order to satisfy His thirst for justice, or for any other kind of legal debt. Again, our salvation is not a legal issue. The Son of God had to die in order to take our sin nature to the grave.

> [24] *And He Himself bore our sins in His body on the cross, so that we might **die** to sin and **live** to righteousness (1 Peter 2:24).*

Due to the law of nature, mortal man cannot be good disconnected from the good God, nor can he live disconnected from the Life Giver. When Adam divorced God in Eden, he severed his connection to the only Source of life and good for all of us. The only way to fix this problem and give Adam and his lost family another chance at life was for them to be reconciled to God. But, remember, the carnal heart is at enmity with God and cannot independently choose to return to Him. Instead, God sent His only Son into the world to join the human race—but with a difference. While Jesus fully inherited Adam's fallen *flesh,* a human body ravaged by four thousand years of sin, His nature was fully divine, that of the only born Son of God the Father.

> *[14] And the Word became flesh, and dwelt among us, and we saw His glory, glory as of the only begotten from the Father, full of grace and truth (John 1:14).*

Stripped of the supernatural *attributes* or powers of divinity (omnipotence, omnipresence, omniscience), Jesus kept the *nature* of divinity, that being, divinity alone is good. By nature, His instinct was to love righteousness and hate iniquity (sin). Thus, the Man Jesus was able to choose to return to God in Adam's stead because He was not carnal in His spiritual nature and, therefore, not at enmity with God—and that is what makes Him a real Superhero![1]

---

[1] Omni means *all,* so, omnipotence is all-powerful; omnipresence is all-present; omniscience is all-knowing; Philippians 2:5–8; Hebrews 1:8, 9.

7

Supernatural Power to Set Us Free!

et's consider another mistaken belief: that sinners cannot exist in the presence of a pure and holy God. When we correctly understand the true nature of the Supreme God and His all-present Spirit, we will recognize that, though not *in* everything, God is always *everywhere*.

> [23] *"Am I a God who is near,"* declares the LORD, *"and not a God far off?"* [24] *"Can a man hide himself in hiding places so I do not see him?"* declares the LORD. *"Do I not fill the heavens and the earth?"* declares the LORD (Jeremiah 23:23, 24).

> [7] *Where can I go from Your Spirit? Or where can I flee from Your presence?* [8] *If I ascend into heaven, You are*

there; If I make my bed in hell, behold, You are there (Psalm 139:7, 8 NKJV).

[27] But will God indeed dwell on the earth? Behold, heaven and the highest heaven cannot contain You, how much less this house which I have built! (1 Kings 8:27)

Is there anywhere in all the vast creation that God Almighty does not exist or any corner of the universe that He does not fill? He does not withhold Himself even where the deepest, darkest, most toxic evil hides. If He did, it would cease to exist! God upholds every created thing: Satan himself is sustained by Him, breath by breath. However, it's the glory of God that corrupt beings cannot look upon and live.[1]

God's presence is everywhere. Remember, it is not a "force" or "power", but *the very life, the very person of God the Father Himself,* but in Spirit form. John 4:24 says, "God is spirit". Again, using basic grammar, we can understand that God's state of being is Spirit. His person, His mind, His thoughts, His feelings—everything that makes God the Father who He is—is Spirit, and His Spirit fills the universe. His physical form is visible, while His Spirit is invisible.

King David understood this crucial truth. He identified the Spirit as "the God of Israel" and "the Rock of Israel."

*[2] The **Spirit of the LORD spoke** through me, And His word was on my tongue. [3] The **God of Israel said** it; The **Rock of Israel spoke** to me (2 Samuel 23:2, 3).*

Over 120 Bible verses identify "the LORD," Jehovah, also known as Yah or Yahweh, as "the God of Israel". He *alone* is

---

[1] Job 12:10; 33:4; 34:14, 15; Psalm 145:9; Acts 17:28; Hebrews 4:13; 1 Timothy 6:15, 16; Exodus 33:20, 23.

God "Most High" over all creation, the One who sits on the throne of heaven—and no one else.[1]

> [15] *Hezekiah prayed before the* Lord *and said,* **"Lord, God of Israel,** *enthroned above the cherubim [angels],* **You are the God, You alone,** *of all the kingdoms of the earth. You have made heaven and earth (2 Kings 19:15).*

By definition, if something or someone is the *most* anything, there is no thing or being greater or equal. Only one can be "most."

> [18] *That they may know that* **You alone,** *whose name is the* Lord, *are the Most High over all the earth (Psalm 83:18).*

God never does anything randomly. He established the laws of nature as they are for a reason: They are based upon a divine model. Recall that the law of inheritance states that everything produces after its kind. God Himself brought forth His Son after His kind, meaning, Christ inherited His Father's divine nature. Before anything was ever created, the Son of God was *begotten* as "the exact representation of His [Father's] nature" (Hebrews 1:3). Indeed, "The Son is the image of the invisible God, the *firstborn* over all creation" (Colossians 1:15 NIV).[2]

> [10] *He who descended is Himself also He who ascended far above all the heavens, so* **that He might fill all things** *(Ephesians 4:10).*

---

[1] "Lord" is a substitute for the name of God, versus "Lord," which means *master*. Deuteronomy 4:35; 32:39; Nehemiah 9:6; Isaiah 43:10; 44:6–8; 45:6; Revelation 4:2, 3, etc.
[2] John 8:42; 17:8.

As God's Son, Jesus is also Spirit. This means the Spirit of Jesus is *the very person of Jesus Christ Himself.* His Father then *"established"* Him with divine supernatural powers. See Proverbs 8:23–25. Because these powers were granted, they could be given back in order to become a Man.

Though Jesus was "emptied" of His divine *powers*—the "omnis"—during His life as a Man, His divine nature is not in question—He is, after all, the begotten—not created—Son of the Most High. We know this because God Himself said so—twice. And God cannot lie. We also know that God *sent* His only begotten Son into the world. We know this because Jesus Himself said so. And He never lied. More importantly, for God to *send* His Son *into* the world He had to have a Son first to send. Jesus said (1) He "came forth from the Father" and (2) "have come into the world" (John 16:28). Nowhere does the Bible say that God, in any form, came into the world to *become* the Son. We are told God *gave* His only Son, or *sent* His Son, into the world—the ultimate Gift. The reason was so "He might fill all things."[1]

God the Father is the one God of the Bible. He is called the *Father* because He is the Father of Jesus. He is also the God of Jesus.[2]

> [3] *Blessed be the God and Father of our Lord Jesus Christ (2 Corinthians 1:3).*

> [3] *Grace, mercy and peace will be with us, from God the Father and from Jesus Christ, the Son of the Father, in truth and love (2 John 1:3).*

In addition, "God is the head of Christ" (1 Corinthians 11:3), making Him alone the God-head. God the Father is

---

[1] Philippians 2:7; *Beget* (begotten): Isaiah 39:7; Matthew 17:5; Titus 1:2; John 3:17.
[2] Mark 5:7; John 20:17; 2 Corinthians 11:31; Proverbs 30:4.

supreme over *all*. As the omnipotent God, He has no limitations.[1]

> [23] *And you belong to Christ, and Christ belongs to God (1 Corinthians 3:23).*

The Bible is quite clear also when it comes to the Spirit: There is only one Spirit. Since God the Father is that one Spirit, when He anointed His Son with His Spirit, it was done in such a way that it still makes one Spirit. As far as the Bible is concerned, such as in Romans 8:9, the Spirit of God and the Spirit of Christ are interchangeable.[2]

> [17] *But the one who joins himself to the Lord is one spirit with Him (1 Corinthians 6:17).*

Now, when we read that *in* Christ dwells "all the fullness" of the *Godhead* bodily, it makes more sense. This principle remains true for us as well. Through the miracle of the new birth, the Spirit of the Son, *with* the Spirit of the Father, joins with the spirit of the new believer in such a way that it still makes one spirit: the Father in Christ, and Christ and the Father in us. Literally, but in Spirit.[3]

> [20] *In that day you will know that I am **in** My Father, and you **in** Me, and I **in** you . . .*[23] *Jesus answered and said to him, "If anyone loves Me, he will keep My word; and My Father will love him, and **We** will come to him and make **Our** abode with him (John 14:20, 23).*

---

[1] "Head" means *first* or *chief*. Like the "most", there can only be one "head."

[2] Ephesians 2:18; 4:4; 1 Corinthians 12:13; John 14:10, 11; John 3:34 BSB; Luke 4:18; Matthew 12:18; Acts 10:38.

[3] Colossians 2:9 NKJV.

*²³ I **in** them and You **in** Me, that they may be perfected in unity, so that the world may know that You sent Me, and loved them, even as You have loved Me (John 17:23).*

It's through this supernatural born-again experience that Christ's Spirit joins with our spirit, allowing us to partake of His divine nature. We then inherit His characteristics, including His love of righteousness, delivering us from the bondage of the nature of sin! This is our *new* inheritance!

*⁴ For by these He has granted to us His precious and magnificent promises, so that by them you may become **partakers of the divine nature,** having escaped the corruption that is in the world by lust (2 Peter 1:4).*

*⁹ No one born of God commits sin; for God's **nature** abides in him, and he cannot sin because he is born of God (1 John 3:9 RSV).*

Because Jesus is free from sin, we can be free from sin *in* Him!

³⁶ So if the Son makes you free, you will be free indeed (John 8:36).

8
The Only Superhero
We'll Ever Need

As the only ever real-life Superhero, Jesus is the only One who can bring the power of God beyond the physical realm into the spiritual, into our hearts and minds: We become perfect in spirit because He is perfect in Spirit. It's through our relationship with God through His Son that the visible fruits of the Spirit—love, joy, peace, etc.—will flow naturally out of us like "rivers of living water" (John 7:38; see also Galatians 5:22, 23).

Having the unblemished divine-human life of Jesus alive in us will naturally change how we relate to the world around us. Our new instinct will be to "walk in love" with the gentleness and purity of Christ. See Ephesians 5:2.

*¹¹ Having been filled with the fruit of righteousness which comes **through** Jesus Christ (Philippians 1:11).*

This is why it is essential to understand *who* the holy Spirit really is, and why anything that teaches otherwise is utterly destructive to our salvation.

The majority of Christians have been taught to believe in a third divine being called *God the Holy Spirit,* defined as either another Person within the *same substance* of God or the third member of a *unity* called God: *God the Father, God the Son, and God the Holy Spirit.* Some explain it as one God manifesting Himself as Father before Bethlehem, as Jesus during His life on earth, and as Holy Spirit after Pentecost. Others explain it as three different Beings who are "one" in the sense of purpose. To embrace this and still hold to the Bible's strict doctrine of only one God requires some creative accounting: 1+1+1=1, not 3.[1]

While the Bible plainly teaches there's only one God, it actually reveals two physical divine Beings: Father and Son. For instance, Daniel 7 is a vision of the judgment with the Son of Man [Son of God] coming to the Ancient of Days [the Father]. Three times, the Father spoke to Jesus from heaven proclaiming Him to be His Son. Jesus said He could do nothing of Himself, but that His Father did the works, and repeatedly said He had been *sent* by the Father; Jesus on earth prayed to the Father in heaven; Revelation 4:4 shows God on the throne and Jesus as the Lamb taking the scroll from His hand; etc. None of this makes any sense if Jesus was sent by Himself, coming to Himself, or talking to, or about, Himself. And the idea of three distinct divine Beings is firmly not biblical.[2]

Who then is this third entity, *God the Holy Spirit?* Con-

---

[1] Mark 12:29. Note: The terms *God the Son* and *God the Holy Spirit* are not biblical and will be noted in italics; only the term "God the Father" is biblical, as is "Son of God", and "Spirit of God" or "Spirit of Christ."
[2] Daniel 7:13; Matthew 3:17; 17:5; John 4:24; 5:19, 30; 6:37; 10:36; 12:28; John 17; Revelation 5:6, 7; Galatians 4:4.

sider that *God the Holy Spirit* does not have a victorious divine-human experience to give to us. Jesus does. *God the Holy Spirit* was not tempted in all points like we are. Jesus was. *God the Holy Spirit* cannot come to the aid of those who are tempted because he too had been tempted. Jesus can, because Jesus was. We cannot die with *God the Holy Spirit,* be buried in his death, and raised up with him into new life, because this *God the Holy Spirit* did not die, was not buried, and was not raised up in triumphant glory. We can experience these things only in Christ Jesus.

> *[17] Now **the Lord [Jesus] is the Spirit,** and where the Spirit of the Lord is, there is liberty (2 Corinthians 3:17).*

Only Jesus could accomplish all this on our behalf precisely because He is the only begotten Son of God who became one with humanity. Divine in Spirit, human in fallen flesh, Jesus heroically gained victory over the flesh and sin nature and now melds that experience into our own human existence through the indwelling of His own victorious life.[1]

> *[20] I have been crucified with Christ; and it is no longer I who live, but **Christ lives in me;** and the life which I now live in the flesh I live by faith in the Son of God, who loved me and gave Himself up for me (Galatians 2:20).*

Also consider that the disciples never baptized in the name(s) of the Father, Son, and Holy Spirit. They baptized only in the name of the Lord Jesus Christ because baptism represents the death, burial, and resurrection of Jesus. Not even God the Father experienced that.[2]

---

[1] Hebrews 2:18; 4:15; 5:8, 9; Luke 13:32 NKJV.
[2] Acts 8:16; 10:48; 19:5; thus, question the common view of Matthew 28:19.

38 Peter said to them, "Repent, and each of you be baptized in the name of Jesus Christ for the forgiveness of your sins; and you will receive the gift of the Holy Spirit (Acts 2:38).

Only in Jesus—His victory over sin, His righteousness, His sanctification and redemption, His power and wisdom, His peace, His love—all perfected in human flesh—is everything we need for salvation. Because Jesus possesses everything we need to be saved, we possess everything we need: We are complete *in* Him, lacking *nothing*.

*10 And **in Him** you have been made complete [already!], and He is the head over all rule and authority (Colossians 2:10).*

We receive it all through the inheritance of adoption by being born again into Jesus and into the royal family of God. Only divine supernatural Power could accomplish this!

15 You received the Spirit of adoption by whom we cry out, "Abba, Father" (Romans 8:15 NKJV).

Jesus doesn't just *give* us righteousness; He doesn't *cover* us in righteousness—He *is* our righteousness. Out of the abundance of the heart, doing right from the inside out, it is Christ living His own transforming life *in* us!

*28 We proclaim Him, admonishing every man and teaching every man with all wisdom, so that we may present every man **complete in** Christ. 29 For this purpose also I labor, striving according to His power, which mightily works **within** me (Colossians 1:28, 29).*

Adam sold us under sin, but in His immeasurable love for us God did not leave mankind to die under the curse of Adam's choice. Jesus Christ purchased our freedom with His own blood and renews us with His life.

> [28] *Be on guard for yourselves and for all the flock, among which the* **Holy Spirit** *has made you over-seers, to shepherd the church of God which* **He [the Holy Spirit (subject)] purchased with His own blood** *(Acts 20:28).*

Our hearts should burst with eternal gratitude for this "victory through our Lord Jesus Christ" (1 Corinthians 15:57).

9

The Good News of the Kingdom

In these closing hours of earth's history, God has been revealing a clearer understanding of Christ as our Righteousness through the concept of the two Adams and the laws of heredity. And now He is bringing to light a better understanding of the "gospel of the kingdom."

> *¹ Now in those days John the Baptist came, preaching in the wilderness of Judea, saying, ² "Repent, for the kingdom of heaven is at hand" (Matthew 3:1, 2).*

From the time of John the Baptist, the message was preached that the "kingdom of heaven" was at hand. The kingdom of heaven is mentioned more than a dozen times just in the book of Matthew, plus other references to the "kingdom of God." John the Baptist preached it. Jesus preached it. The disciples were instructed to preach it. Jesus spoke many parables illustrating the kingdom of heaven.[1]

> [14] This **gospel of the kingdom** shall be preached in the whole world as a testimony to all the nations, and then the end will come (Matthew 24:14).

It is *this* gospel, this good news of "the kingdom," that we are to proclaim to all the world before the end can come. Many believe the kingdom of God is where we go after the Second Coming when the saints are redeemed from the earth. But there's just one hitch to that.[2]

> [21] Nor will they say, 'See here!' or 'See there!' For indeed, **the kingdom of God is within you"** (Luke 17:21 NKJV).

> [17] For the kingdom of God is not eating and drinking, but **righteousness** and **peace** and **joy** in the Holy Spirit (Romans 14:17).

It is true there is a literal kingdom in heaven and in the earth-made-new where the ransomed will live for eternity. But if the kingdom of God is *within* us, it cannot only be a destination, but also a way of life. This *Way of Life* is our passport into the physical kingdom of heaven.

Knowing that Jesus is, among other things, our Way and our Life (see John 14:6), we come into the kingdom of God when Christ comes to reign on the throne of our hearts and minds through His Spirit. Then we will do God's will here "on earth as it is in heaven" (Matthew 6:9, 10).

Consider this: God was known in the Old Testament as Je-

---

[1] Matthew 4:17; 5:3, 10, 19, 20; 9:35; 10:5–7; 13:24, 31, etc.
[2] The return of Jesus will not be "secret": Acts 1:9–11; Revelation 1:7; Matthew 16:27; 24:27–31; 1 Thessalonians 4:16.

hovah, the self-existent all-powerful God, in contrast to the man-made powerless idols the nations worshipped. When Jesus came, His mission was to reveal a side of God not previously known by instructing us to address God as *Father*. What a thought! The Infinite Ruler of the universe wants us to relate to Him as our Father![1]

God's new covenant name—Father—is what the end-time believers will have "written on their foreheads" (Revelation 14:1). It signifies they have a family relationship with the Divine and are members in His kingdom.[2]

> [7] *For God hath not given us the spirit of fear; but of* **power,** *and of* **love,** *and of a* **sound mind** *(2 Timothy 1:7 KJV).*

> [16] *That He would grant you, according to the riches of His glory, to be strengthened* **with power** *through His Spirit in the inner man (Ephesians 3:16).*

The kingdom of God is the divine life of *Christ-in-you* in power and authority. However, God is not the only one with a kingdom.

---

[1] Jehovah, God the Father, has 100-plus names and titles in the OT, each meant to reveal a different aspect of His great character, and not so much about a specific word by which we are to refer to Him. In the OT, Creator is a name/title that most identifies Him apart from all other gods (Isaiah 44:24); John 17:26.

[2] Revelation 22:4.

10

A Rival Kingdom

There are two opposing powers, or kingdoms, battling for supremacy in this world: the power of God in Christ and the power of Satan.[1]

The cosmic controversy has pitted the kingdom of Satan and his form of government against the kingdom of God the Father and His form of government. And despite what anyone prefers to believe, there is no such thing as the *Kingdom of the Fence;* there is no neutral territory in this war, just as there is no dual citizenship. You can be a citizen of only one of these kingdoms—not both, and not neither.

Now, to answer that million-dollar question of why God doesn't intervene more often in the tragedies of life. While there are several factors, the primary reason is that this world isn't His kingdom. Satan became the legitimate ruler of this planet when he overthrew Adam in the Garden of Eden. Since

---

[1] Matthew 12:25–28.

then, as the rival ruler and reigning Evil Emperor of planet earth, he alone is responsible for making a deplorable shipwreck of this once perfect creation.[1]

> *⁵ And he led Him up and showed Him **all the kingdoms of the world** in a moment of time. ⁶ And the devil said to Him, "I will give You **all this domain** and its glory, for **it has been handed over to me,** and I give it to whomever I wish (Luke 4:5, 6).*

> *² According to the course of this world, according to the prince of the power of the air, of the spirit that is now working in the sons of disobedience (Ephesians 2:2).*

Before rebelling against the Most High, Satan was Lucifer, the *Lightbearer,* a special covering angel standing in the presence of God Himself. He was created perfectly pure and, like every other noble being God created, was given free will. That freedom of choice is what led to the great mystery of iniquity. Lucifer chose a path other than God's; he chose to rebel against Jehovah, and deceived a staggering number of the angels of heaven into following him.[2]

> *¹² You were the seal of perfection, full of wisdom and perfect in beauty. ¹³ You were in Eden, the garden of God. . . . ¹⁴ You were the anointed cherub who covers; I established you. . . . ¹⁵ You were perfect in your ways from the day you were created, Till iniquity was found in you. ¹⁶ By the abundance of your trading you became filled with violence within, and you sinned (Ezekiel 28:12–16 NKJV).*

---

[1] Ephesians 6:12; Job 1:6, 7; 2:1, 2; 1 Kings 22:19–23.
[2] Revelation 12:3, 4, 9.

*[12] How you are fallen from heaven, O Lucifer, son of the morning! How you are cut down to the ground, you who weakened the nations! [13] For you have said in your heart: I will ascend into heaven, I will exalt my throne above the stars of God; I will also sit on the mount of the congregation on the farthest sides of the north; [14] I will ascend above the heights of the clouds, **I will be like the Most High** (Isaiah 14:12–14).*

Remember that the great principle of creation is that divinity alone is good. It is a major separating factor between the kingdom of Satan and the kingdom of God. Since God the Father is the only Source of life and light, mercy and compassion, and all things honest and good, the absence of God means the absence of all these wondrous things. When Lucifer rejected God, as a created being, he had nothing of his own to offer his loyal subjects except darkness and death, violence and fear, and all things corrupt and vile. On top of that, he's become a master manipulator and deceiver. These are his superpowers.[1]

With him there can be no peace, no goodwill, nothing but disease, mayhem and, in the end, death—in a completely, eternally, void-of-life kind of way. All the deformities and calamities of this life are the responsibility of the Prince of Darkness, and our destruction is the goal of his kingdom—to *kill, steal, and destroy*—and to reign in opposition to the supreme God of the universe permanently. See John 10:10. Satan's kingdom can never come close to the original paradise. Despite this, blame for every horrendous thing the world has ever witnessed has consistently been hurled at the face of God.

Though this is now a villain's domain, God still sits on His throne: He has prevented Doctor Death from destroying everything and everyone in it, while graciously allowing this

---

[1] John 8:44.

grand deceiver to make his case against Him and His government. Thus, we can see these two opposing forces at work every day. We see beauty in nature, and we see decay and ruin;
we know peace and joy, and we know pain and suffering. We
are alive to experience these things because the Living God
sustains us breath by breath and has intervened to protect us
from the Destroyer. At the same time, God is working to draw
us back to Himself through a revelation of His true character
by breaking the spell of this Master Wizard.[1]

> [45] *For He causes His sun to rise on the evil and the good,
> and sends rain on the righteous and the unrighteous
> (Matthew 5:45).*

The great hallmark of Satan's kingdom is *death.* It is one
of mankind's greatest enemies. It separates us from those we
love and can eventually separate us from life permanently.
However, the death that people experience today is not the
permanent one. The Bible calls this form of death *sleep.* Just
as the living can fall into a deep sleep and not realize anything
until morning, so the dead have no thoughts, no feelings, and
no reward.[2]

> [5] *For the living know they will die; but the dead do not
> know anything, nor have they any longer a reward, for
> their memory is forgotten.* [6] *Indeed their love, their hate
> and their zeal have already perished, and they will no
> longer have a share in all that is done under the sun.*
> [10] *Whatever your hand finds to do, do it with all your
> might; for there is no activity or planning or knowledge
> or wisdom in Sheol [the grave] where you are going
> (Ecclesiastes 9:5, 6, 10).*

---

[1] Job 10:12; Isaiah 42:5; Psalm 91:5–12; Acts 14:17.
[2] John 11:11–14; Mark 5:39; Psalm 13:3; Ephesians 5:14, etc.

*[14] The dead will not live, **the departed spirits will not rise;** therefore You have punished and destroyed them, and You have wiped out all remembrance of them (Isaiah 26:14).*

Death is not a state of being. Death is the *absence* of the state of being alive; it is separation from life. Both the righteous and wicked dead have no consciousness in the grave and are not aware of their condition. They neither become angels in heaven nor disembodied spirits tormented in hell. Our dearly departed are not watching us or interfering in our lives. God has given us peace to know that, for now, the dead are asleep in the grave, awaiting their future reward.[1]

[28] Do not marvel at this; for an hour is coming, in which all who are in the tombs will hear His voice, [29] and will come forth; *those who did the good deeds to a resurrection of life, those who committed the evil deeds to a resurrection of judgment (John 5:28, 29).*

[2] Many of those who sleep in the dust of the ground will awake, these to everlasting life, but the others to disgrace and everlasting contempt (Daniel 12:2).

Clearly, God told Adam and Eve they would "surely die" if they ate the forbidden fruit—not because He would kill them, but because they would become separated from His life. Thus, it is not possible that only their bodies would die while their spirits continued to live in an altered state. Death, again, is the absence of life. Satan was a master at convincing Eve that God was a liar and they would not die. That lie has become the foundation of his kingdom of Deceit, and it has been thriving until this very day.[2]

---

[1] Psalm 6:5; 115:17; 146:4; Isaiah 38:18, 19; Acts 24:15.
[2] Genesis 2:17; 3:4; Romans 3:4.

Do not be deceived: death is real and complete. And though it is still death, and for most unavoidable, it is not the final story.

> [19] *For the fate of the sons of men and the fate of beasts is the same. As one dies so dies the other; indeed, they all have the same breath and there is no advantage for man over beast, for all is vanity.* [20] *All go to the same place. All came from the dust and all return to the dust.* [21] *Who knows that the **breath** of man ascends upward and the breath of the beast descends downward to the earth? (Ecclesiastes 3:19–21).*

Adam should have died the day he sinned, and that would have been the end of the story for him and the human race. But God was prepared. In His immense love and wisdom, He immediately activated Operation Plan of Salvation which extended Adam's life and allowed his eventual death to become temporary. When Adam died at 930 years, his body returned to the dust and his breath returned to God, as warned. While his *identity* has been preserved, Adam himself ceased to exist.

Four thousand years later, the Seed of the woman, Jesus, came and "bruised" the serpent's head, making possible the resurrection. Soon, Jesus will return to restore Adam's life and clothe him in a glorious new body. So it is with all who sleep in Jesus.[1]

> [17] *For if, by the trespass of the one man [Adam], death reigned through that one man, how much more will those who receive God's abundant provision of grace and of the gift of righteousness reign in life through the one man, Jesus Christ! (Romans 5:17 NIV).*

---

[1] Genesis 3:14–19; 5:5.

It is the Second Death, the one that comes after the Second Coming of Jesus, after the final judgment, which is the permanent separation from life and the Giver of it. This death is the one we can actually avoid by receiving Jesus Christ and His eternal life. To be specific, *there is only one Man Who is worthy to be saved,* and all those who desire salvation and eternal life must be in that one Man, Jesus.

Until then, our ultimate purpose is not length of days in this marred creation, but to come to know God through a personal relationship with Him so that we may experience a better life now and for all eternity—and avoid the second death.[1]

> [6] *Blessed and holy is the one who has a part in the first resurrection; over these the **second death** has no power (Revelation 20:6).*

But the Dark Deceiver has managed to corrupt our knowledge of God's selfless character of love to the extent that the majority of professed Christians today see our heavenly Father as capable of deliberately *sustaining* the lives of sinners—His own wayward children—in the flames of hell, just so He can torture them for all eternity.

This is a horrific insult to the One the Bible calls *Love.* What father with an ounce of compassion could stoop to such savagery just because his children disobey him? Are *rules* so much more precious in God's sight than His own sons and daughters? Never! This kind of thinking is the result of believing our problem with sin is *legal* and not *nature*—and that God loves justice more than His children. This is the ultimate legalism.

> [11] *Say to them: "As I live," says the Lord GOD, "I have no pleasure in the death of the wicked, but that the wicked turn from his way and live. Turn, turn from your evil*

---
[1] Acts 17:24–28; Isaiah 55:6, 7.

*ways! For why should you die, O house of Israel?"
(Ezekiel 33:11 NKJV).*

³² *"For I have no pleasure in the death of anyone who
dies," declares the Lord* GOD. *"Therefore, repent and
live"! (Ezekiel 18:32).*

It is not even possible for the Father of all creation to be
that demented. In all honesty, that kind of twisted "justice"
rightfully belongs to Satan. Eternal death is not God's choice
for the wicked, but their own. Those who reject Jesus Christ
and the eternal Life He offers cannot live in their own power—
and Satan has no life to offer. And forget this desperate non-
sense that man can have immortality through transhuman-
ism!

Rightfully said is the proverb that all who hate God "love
death" (Proverbs 8:36). Soon, God will honor their desire to
be fully separated from Him and they will die, eternally severed from Life, never to exist again.

Know with clear certainty that the wages of sin is *death*.
The wages of sin is *not* eternal life, *especially* not in torment.
Eternal life is the free gift of God reserved only for those who
are *in* the Last Adam, Jesus Christ.

²³ *For the wages of sin is death, but the free gift of God is
eternal life in Christ Jesus our Lord (Romans 6:23).*

11

How the Superhero Defeated the Villain

This brings us to our Superhero's side of this controversy: the government of God. God the Father has professed His own character and government to be the one of utmost integrity:

> *6 Then the LORD . . . proclaimed, "The LORD, the LORD God, compassionate and gracious, slow to anger, and abounding in lovingkindness and truth; 7 who keeps lovingkindness for thousands, who forgives iniquity, transgression and sin; yet He will by no means leave the guilty unpunished, visiting the iniquity of fathers on the children and on the grandchildren to the third and fourth generations" (Exodus 34:6, 7).*

These are God's superpowers. More so, they are part of what makes God who He is, that is, His state of being, His nature. Nevertheless, Jehovah God has been charged with crimes against creation by the Arch-Accuser. God Himself is the one on trial, and in this case, Self-defense is not the best defense. Considering the accusations, God needed a defender, a personal witness. Naturally, His Son is the best Representative to defend the character of God and His government. As a Man on earth, Jesus perfectly demonstrated His Father's faultless character before all creation by dealing with mankind's open rebellion with love and patience.[1]

> *[14] Glory to God in the highest, and on earth peace, good will toward men! (Luke 2:14 NKJV).*

> *[11] For I know the thoughts that I think toward you, says the LORD, thoughts of peace and not of evil, to give you a future and a hope (Jeremiah 29:11 NKJV).*

God's goal was to intercept man on his path to self-destruction. By sending His own Son to become a Son of Adam, God was able to re-introduce into the stream of humanity what had been lost. Jesus faultlessly relayed the Father's goodwill for the people: healing their diseases, calming their fears, raising their dead, and casting out demonic foes—always echoing the compassion and mercy and love of God toward us.

> *[38] You know of Jesus of Nazareth, how God anointed Him with the Holy Spirit and with power, and how He went about doing good and healing all who were oppressed by the devil, for God was with Him (Acts 10:38).*

---
[1] Isaiah 9:6.

It was this selfless heart of love that Evil Lord Satan—working through like-minded men willing to put their own interests above all else—nailed to a brutal cross in an attempt to exterminate the Prince of Peace. As Jesus was consumed by the cruelty of the cross, He was placed where *we* deserved to be—right where Adam put us: abandoned by all earthly help, stripped naked, scourged mercilessly, and left alone by God in Satan's hands.[1]

[18] Now all these things are from God, who reconciled us to Himself through Christ and gave us the ministry of reconciliation, [19] namely, that God was in Christ reconciling the world to Himself, not counting their trespasses against them, and He has committed to us the word of reconciliation. . . . [20] We beg you on behalf of Christ, be reconciled to God. [21] He made Him who knew no sin to be sin on our behalf (2 Corinthians 5:18–21).

On the cross, Jesus Christ reconciled the whole world to God by being made sin for us. This doesn't mean He was made into an act of disobedience against the law. It means, like Adam, He was separated from God. As He hung from the agonizing nails, His Father turned away from Him—something Jesus had never before experienced nor expected: "MY GOD, MY GOD, WHY HAVE YOU FORSAKEN ME?" (Mark 15:34) We can only imagine how it crushed the Father's tender heart as He must deliberately turn away from His beloved Son, all while hearing His desperate plea for a response and watching His shocked reaction.

In that brief moment, the innocent Son of God experienced what it's like to be totally without God. Immediately, demons had full access and descended on Him like an overflowing torrent. Deep, penetrating darkness entered His pure mind, the horror of what it means to be truly void of God:

---

[1] Acts 2:23.

black emotions, a flood of temptations, hopelessness. Yet, Jesus did what none of us have ever been able to do—Jesus was separated from the good God, but did not turn to self. In the shadow of eternal death, His unpolluted heart was sustained by absolute faith: "Father, forgive them" (Luke 23:34). *This was His greatest superpower!*

This was possible only because He is the divine Son of God with a nature that loves righteousness and hates sin. Because Jesus received His life from His Father, the only Source of Life, when God separated Himself from His Son, the natural consequence is that Jesus, Son of man and Son of God, died completely.[1]

> [9] *Then they made his grave with the wicked, and with rich people in his death, although he had committed no violence, nor was there any deceit in his mouth.* [10] *Yet the LORD was willing to crush him, and he made him suffer. Although you make his soul an offering for sin, he will see his offspring, and he will prolong his days, and the will of the LORD will triumph in his hand (Isaiah 53:9, 10 ISV).*

What an indescribable sacrifice! And when Jesus died, He took the enmity—our state of hostility toward and separation from God—with Him into death. Through His willing sacrifice, Jesus bore our sins in our place and "redeemed us from the curse of the Law" (Galatians 3:13).[2]

> [22] *For as in Adam all die, so also* **in** *Christ all will be made alive (1 Corinthians 15:22).*

---

[1] John 5:26; 6:57; 1 Timothy 6:13–16.
[2] Luke 23:33–47; Isaiah 53:1–12.

*¹¹ For the L*ORD *has ransomed Jacob and redeemed him from the hand of him who was stronger than he (Jeremiah 31:11).*

The tables were forever turned the day Jesus defeated Satan on the cross. Casting the innocent Son of God into the grave was not the victory the Devil thought he had achieved. Rather, it marked his doom. Through the cross the character of the divine God of heaven was vindicated as being just and righteous under any and all circumstances. And because Death had no authority to keep the Sinless One separated from His Father, God had all rights to reclaim Him from the dead. When Jesus left the grave, He took the keys of death with Him and broke its power forever![1]

¹⁷ I am the first and the last, ¹⁸ and the living One; and I was dead, and behold, I am alive forevermore, and I have the keys of death and of Hades (Revelation 1:17, 18).

The Man Jesus Christ has reclaimed the dominion that Satan manipulated away from Adam. In a fatal twist of irony, the Empire of Death that Satan built has been given its own eternal death sentence. Praise Almighty God! It's only a matter of time before his sentence is carried out.[2]

²⁶ The last enemy to be destroyed is death (1 Corinthians 15:26 NIV).

¹⁴ Then Death and Hades were cast into the lake of fire. This is the second death. ¹⁵ And anyone not found written in the Book of Life was cast into the lake of fire. (Revelation 20:14, 15 NKJV).

---

[1] 1 Peter 2:22; Deuteronomy 32:4; Acts 2:22-24.
[2] Daniel 7:19–27.

The good news for us is that this conquest of the ages is for all—every person who has ever been born. The victory is already won. All condemnation and shame are forever removed. All any of us has to do is just accept this beautiful gift and step over onto the winning side.

> *[2] And he [Christ] is the atoning sacrifice for our sins, and not for ours only but* **also for the sins of the whole world** *(1 John 2:2 NRSV).*

> *[14] We have seen and testify that the Father has sent the Son to be the Savior of the world (1 John 4:14).*

Just as predicted, the Superhero wins and the Villain loses. But even that's not the end of the story.

12
The Superhero Returns

I t is generally believed that salvation was finished at the cross. Jesus's death on Calvary was indeed tragically necessary in order to *reconcile,* or reunite, us to God. But strange as it may seem, reconciliation was not enough. We are actually "saved by His life" (Romans 5:10).

Fifty days after the resurrection of Jesus a new kingdom, a counter-kingdom, was established on the earth: the kingdom of God and Christ. Pentecost launched this new era, marked by flaming tongues of fire, a fitting symbol of the new church: "And they were all filled with the Holy Spirit" (Acts 2:4). This is when Jesus returned to His disciples in Spirit form.

> *[19] Repent therefore and be converted, that your sins may be blotted out, so that **times of refreshing** may come from the presence of the Lord, [20] and that **He may send Jesus Christ,** who was preached to you*

before. ²⁶ *To you first, God, having raised up His Servant **Jesus, sent Him** to bless you, in turning away every one of you from your iniquities (Acts 3:19, 20, 26 NKJV).*

Through the outpouring of His Spirit, the risen Redeemer came back to earth in superhuman Power, infusing the believers with His own presence and transforming them in power from the inside out. Jesus Christ was living in human flesh again, not in one body, but in many!

³ *And every spirit that confesseth not that Jesus Christ **is come in the flesh** is not of God: and this is that spirit of antichrist, whereof ye have heard that it should come; and even now already is it in the world (1 John 4:3 KJV).*

Since Pentecost, Jesus Christ has been serving as our High Priest, ministering His own *blood,* that is, His *life* (Leviticus 17:11), not in an earthly temple of stone or even a heavenly temple of gold, but in our hearts and minds. This is the stunning truth of the gospel—*we* are the temple that God has chosen as His dwelling place.

¹⁶ *For we are the temple of the living God; just as God said, "I will dwell **in** them and walk among them; and I will be their God, and they shall be My people (2 Corinthians 6:16).*

¹⁶ *Do you not know that you are a temple of God and that the Spirit of God dwells **in** you? (1 Corinthians 3:16).*

In order for us to be complete and functioning according to God's purpose as His dwelling place, we must have Jesus Christ within us, and no one else, for only He qualifies. It was for this purpose that Jesus had to become a Man, so that He could become a faithful High Priest—for only a man can be a priest, and only a priest can enter into the temple.[1]

> *[17] Therefore, He had to be made like His brothers in all things, so that He might become a merciful and faithful high priest in things pertaining to God, to make propitiation [have mercy] for the sins of the people (Hebrews 2:17).*

But, again, for this to be possible we must be born again.

> *[1] Everyone who believes that Jesus is the Christ is born of God, and everyone who loves the father loves his child as well (1 John 5:1 NIV).*

The ultimate battle over sin and death was finalized 2,000 years ago. Everything it took to gain the mastery over Satan and the carnal nature that has chained humanity to sin for millennia has been freely provided. We are all beneficiaries of this great conquest.

> *[1] Therefore there is now* **no condemnation** *for those who are* **in** *Christ Jesus.* *[2] For the law of the Spirit of life* **in** *Christ Jesus has set you free from the law of sin and of death (Romans 8:1, 2).*

Because God doesn't condemn us, we can "come boldly to the throne of grace, that we may [always!] obtain mercy and find grace" (Hebrews 4:16 NKJV). We can then experience this life of love and victory to the point that, like the disciples, others will marvel and recognize that we have been with Jesus. But we must believe it as God promised it. *Faith,* then, is

---

[1] Hebrews 9:11, 12, 15.

the key that opens the windows of heaven to receive all the blessings that God has already provided in His dear Son.[1]

> [20] *And He said to them . . . "truly I say to you, if you have faith the size of a mustard seed, you will say to this mountain, 'Move from here to there,' and it will move; and nothing will be impossible to you" (Matthew 17:20; see also 21:21).*

> [6] *And without faith it is impossible to please God, because anyone who comes to him must believe that he exists and that he rewards those who earnestly seek him (Hebrews 11:6 NIV).*

Faith is believing that God exists, that He has a real Son, and that He has provided all the help we need in that Son if we sincerely seek Him. Faith does not *shrink back* in doubt. See Hebrews 10:38.

Ah, but even this supernatural Superhero has His Kryptonite: Unbelief can bind our Hero from using His superpowers on our behalf. The cure is persistent faith and trust in Christ, without doubting, even when we're tested, even when we don't understand. Do we believe?

> [17] *These signs will accompany those who have believed: in My name they will cast out demons, they will speak with new tongues;* [18] *they will pick up serpents, and if they drink any deadly poison, it will not hurt them; they will lay hands on the sick, and they will recover (Mark 16:17, 18).*

God is calling us to a higher experience. If we are not yet experiencing complete victory over self and openly living in

---

[1] Jude 1:20, 21; Acts 4:13; Hebrews 3:12; Galatians 3:11, 12.

the power of the Spirit, it must be either our lack of understanding or our lack of faith.

> *¹⁸ Little children, let us not love with word or with tongue, but in deed and truth. ¹⁹ We will know by this that we are of the truth, and will assure our heart before Him ²⁰ in whatever our heart condemns us; for God is greater than our heart and knows all things. ²¹ Beloved, if our heart does not condemn us, we have confidence before God; ²² and whatever we ask we receive from Him, because we keep His commandments and do the things that are pleasing in His sight. ²³ **This is His commandment,** that we believe in the name of His Son Jesus Christ, and love one another, just as He commanded us. ²⁴ The one who keeps His commandments abides **in** Him, and He **in** him. **We know by this** that He abides **in** us, by the Spirit whom He has given us (1 John 3:18–24).*

If there is a formula for experiencing the triumphant life of the saints, 1John 3:18–24 is it. It boils down to whether or not we live in an active *relationship* with God and His Son Jesus. Without this intimate connection we will either battle guilt and shame or we will harden our hearts to suppress those feelings, because without Him we will fail. Every. Time.

In our humanity, we may sometimes try to get by with a superficial relationship with God, assuming God is OK with us as long we don't drink, or party, or do other worldly things, and as long as we show up for church once in a while. Then life happens. We get challenged by things we shouldn't, by carnal influences, by people, by life in general. *They* are giving us a hard time; *they* are being mean; *they* are getting on our nerves. . . There's always an excuse. Whether our spouse, our boss, that car that cut us off in traffic—someone is making our day miserable and we think *they* are the problem and need to change. We may even pray for *them* to be better, to be changed so *our* day will go smoother, when *we* are the one who needs to change. *We* need new nerves. *We* need to be renewed by Jesus.

Since God is love, then if His love abides in us, we become the evidence of His love. Like Jesus, we will live out what God is really like through our own life of unconditional kindness and compassion, regardless of how life is treating us, and especially when others aren't treating us fairly. We'll recognize they haven't had this amazing revelation of God. We'll love them as they are and will want to help them to find their true purpose and the same freedom from sin and condemnation we have found. But how do we find this experience? According to verse 22, by keeping His commandments and doing the things that please Him.

First, *every* instruction from God is a "commandment," even if given only to you, so don't fixate on the commandments written on stone. The last generation of the church of Christ will be known for following the Lamb *wherever* He leads, even if it goes against traditionally accepted beliefs. The bottom line is the sheep know the voice of the Shepherd.

Next, only two commandments are required: (1) believing in the name—authority and character—of Jesus Christ and (2) loving one another. The first is all about the new birth, which is the only way we can ever experience the second.[1]

When we receive Jesus, we also receive His faith, a faith that pleases God—bold and strong—with no fear to shrink back. This frees us to allow Him to work through us to do His will. The evidence will be seen as we re-live the life of Jesus: healing the sick, casting out demons, no worry for anything deadly or dangerous, even raising the dead. Wow! In other words, when His life is within, His works are without. This is our high calling (Philippians 3:14 KJV).

---

[1] Revelation 14:4; John 10:27; Isaiah 30:21

[16] For by Him all things were created, both in the heavens and on earth, visible and invisible, whether thrones or dominions or rulers or authorities—all things have been created through Him and for Him. [17] He is before all things, and in Him all things hold together (Colossians 1:16, 17).

Think about it. The supernatural power that framed the worlds and breathed life into clay was given to the Son of God by the Father.[1] If that same supernatural, miracle-working Power lives in us, then when we speak, He speaks. And when we command diseases to leave and demons to depart, they obey, not because we are anything, but because they recognize Jesus Christ speaking through us. It may be our voice, but it is His *authority and power.*

[23] If you can believe, all things are possible to him who believes (Mark 9:23 NKJV).

Dare we say that with God this is not possible?

[20] Now to Him who is able to do far more abundantly **beyond** *all that we ask or think,* **according to the power that works within us,** *[21] to Him be the glory in the church and in Christ Jesus to all generations forever and ever. Amen (Ephesians 3:20, 21).*

---

[1] 1 Corinthians 8:6; Hebrews 1:2; Matthew 28:18; 11:27; John 14:10.

13
War of the Two Kingdoms

The murder of the Son of God on the cross has exposed to the inhabitants of heaven the true character of Satan and his government, and he has been judged accordingly.

*¹¹ Of judgment, because the prince of this world **is judged** (John 16:11 KJV).*

*³¹ **Now** is the judgment of this world: **now** shall the prince of this world be cast out (John 12:31 KJV).*

⁷ And there was war in heaven: Michael and his angels waging war with the dragon. The dragon and his angels waged war, ⁸ and they were not strong enough, and there was no long a place found for them in heaven. ⁹ And the great dragon was thrown down, the serpent

*of old who is called the devil and Satan, who deceives
the whole world; he was thrown down to the earth, and
his angels were thrown down with him. ¹⁰ Then I heard
a loud voice in heaven, saying, **Now the salvation,
and the power, and the kingdom of our God,
and the authority of his Christ have come,** for the
accuser of our brethren has been thrown down, he who
accuses them before our God day and night (Revelation
12:7–10).*

As a result, since the time of Pentecost the Devil knows
the days of his kingdom are numbered and he is stalking
about with the wrath of a lion looking for all he can devour.

*¹² For this reason, rejoice, O heavens and you who dwell
in them. Woe to the earth and the sea, because the devil
has come down to you, having great wrath, knowing
that he has only a short time (Revelation 12:12).*

*⁸ Be of sober spirit, be on the alert. Your adversary, the
devil, prowls around like a roaring lion, seeking someone
to devour (1 Peter 5:8).*

Even so, it is taking much longer to prove to the inhabitants of earth that the kingdom of Satan is ultimately one of
extinction, a government that must rule by extreme *external
force* because it has no goodness in it, and whose citizens hold
passports stamped with greed, perversion, and self-worship.
They bear a striking resemblance to their depraved king who
plotted to destroy the adored Crown Prince of heaven. This is
life independent of God.

We know the same holds true for the children of the kingdom of Christ. That is, they bear a striking resemblance to
their King. However, these citizens have passports stamped

with love and grace and all the fruits of the Spirit, because they live in the kingdom of the divine Spirit.

> [22] *But the fruit of the Spirit is love, joy, peace, patience, kindness, goodness, faithfulness, [23] gentleness, self-control; against such things there is no law (Galatians 5:22, 23).*

They are in it by choice, not force, and their King rules with a pure heart from within. They naturally produce righteousness because their royal lineage is righteous. So, beware of forged passports!

Thus, the kingdom of Satan has been judged and found wanting, and the kingdom of Christ has been judged worthy to rule for eternity. The stark contrast between the two kingdoms is becoming unmistakably clear.

We are now entering a condition upon planet earth where the populace has more than enough evidence to judge the true nature of this imposter Satan and must choose whether to leave his empire of death.[1]

> [13] *But evil men and impostors will grow worse and worse, deceiving and being deceived (2 Timothy 3:13 NKJV).*

The Dark Lord can "read the room" and the gloves are off. He's no longer working by stealth but is manifesting himself more openly and waxing more violent through his subjects than at any other time in history. The holy Spirit is withdrawing from those who have finalized their rejection of Christ. As a result, we are witnessing with regularity what an uncontrolled carnal heart is capable of. Our culture, void of the Spirit of God, is manifesting that lack in outrageous perversion. They actually "call evil good, and good evil" (Isaiah 5:20). At the same time,

---

[1] Daniel 7:9–14.

this final crisis we are entering is drenched in deceit—so much so, if it were possible, it would deceive "even the elect" of God! (Matthew 24:24; see also Matthew 24:4).

Regardless of the extent of the deceit, even non-believers can see something is horribly wrong with the world. From open occultism to human trafficking, corruption with deception is on every level: our governments, our food, our skies, even our genes—everything. Houston, we have a sin problem. It's to the point that many are "fainting from fear and the expectation of the things which are coming upon the world" (Luke 21:26). Today, there's an ominous sense that we're on the verge of some enormous cataclysm, even while leaders insist it's "peace and safety!"[1]

The true children of God are not fearful in spite all of this because they've had a revelation of their Father and "trust the plan"—God's plan is the *only* plan we should trust. That plan is not to secretly *rapture* us before the tribulation, no more than it was for Daniel to avoid the lion's den or for the three Hebrew worthies to avoid the flames. See Daniel 6:10–23; 3:16–28. We're told to endure *"to the end,"* because our God has made Jesus Lord over the lions and Lord over the flames, and He is Lord over every trial we will ever encounter. He "who always leads us in triumph in Christ, and manifests *through us"* will stand strong *with* us in the hottest flames and the fiercest battle (Matthew 10:22; 2 Corinthians 2:14).

God's plan is to carry us through *"the* great tribulation" (Revelation 7:13, 14), thus proving He can make holy humans from those once evil while validating His government as supremely superior above all others.

In the meantime, God is unfolding His plan for us individually, and collectively as the body of Christ. He too, is manifesting Himself more openly and working more powerfully through His children as they learn what it truly means to be born again and live in spiritual freedom. As we come to fully

---

[1] Revelation 13:14; 18:23; 19:20; 20:3, 8, 10; 1 Thessalonians 5:2–4.

grasp the reality of Christ living His life in us, He will strengthen and deepen our faith until we surrender the government of self over to the government of God through Christ. We will reflect the glory of the Lord through the escalating darkness, so that, whether in light or in night, we will shine brighter than the noonday sun. This is our purpose!

> [1] *Arise, shine; for your light has come, and the glory of the LORD has risen upon you.* [2] *For behold, darkness will cover the earth and deep darkness the peoples; but the LORD will rise upon you and His glory will appear upon you (Isaiah 60:1, 2).*

14

Superhero's Seal or Villain's Mark

With so much going wrong in the world today a new term was recently coined—*polycrisis*. This perfect storm of converging crises has birthed a subculture of "preppers", survivalists gearing up for the collapse of society. Believers, however, should first be Kingdom Preppers, stocking up on faith and storing our treasures in heaven. We have peace of mind knowing we are fully equipped in Christ to survive eternally, no matter the conditions. We see these crises for what they are: the final steps of biblical prophecy. We know normal isn't coming back, Jesus is!

[28] When these things begin to happen, look up and lift up your heads, because your redemption draws near (Luke 21:28 NKJV).

[11] Knowing the time, that it is already the hour for you to awaken from sleep; for now salvation is nearer to us than when we believed (Romans 13:11).

Panic preppers also see this hurricane of crises strengthening, but they don't really know Jesus, so they don't know peace. They think their fate is dependent on how well they've prepared. They're fearful of what's ahead, especially the *Mark of the Beast* and the *Antichrist*. But the Mark they fear belongs to no ordinary Beast. This "Beast" is the last governmental empire, and it has the wrong kind of supernatural power behind it. There is no political or prepper or any human solution.[1]

[2] And the dragon [Satan] gave him [the Beast] his power and his throne, and great authority (Revelation 13:2).

[3] Let no one in any way deceive you, for it will not come unless the apostasy comes first, and the man of lawlessness is revealed, the son of destruction [aka the Antichrist] (2 Thessalonians 2:3).

Just as Jesus represents God the Father's kingdom, the Beast of Revelation 13 represents Satan's kingdom: The government of Satan is at work through this authoritarian Beast system, just as God's government of love is at work through the kingdom of Christ in you.

Bear in mind that the book of Revelation is like a series of

---

[1] Daniel 7:17, 23: prophetic beast = king/kingdom = political empire;
1 Corinthians 1:25; 2:14; James 3:17, 18; John 14:27.

riddles. It is not intended for the scholarly or superficial—it's a code book for the saints. Why? Truth is not discovered, it's *revealed,* and only those with *ears to hear* can hear what the Spirit is saying and will be able to rightly decipher the symbols and events recorded. Thus, what the world commonly believes about the Mark of the Beast, and it's infamous 666, cannot be correct because it cannot hear the Spirit.

To begin to understand the Revelation, it has to first be recognized as a book of symbolism, and this symbolism must be translated: The Lamb is not an actual animal, it represents Jesus; winds represent strife; a woman represents a religious organization, pure versus false, hence, not being defiled with women means staying independent of religious organizations; and so on.[1]

> [11] *He told them, "The secret of the kingdom of God has been given to you. But to those on the outside everything is said in parables [riddles] (Mark 4:11 NIV).*

For instance, most people don't realize there are actually two Beast powers in play at the end: The first Beast comes "up out of the sea" (Revelation 13:1), representing a very populated area. See Revelation 17:15. Conversely, the second Beast comes "up out of the earth" (Revelation 13:11), representing a sparsely populated area. But it's the Image that forces the Mark of the Beast upon the world.

> [15] *And it was given to him [earthly Beast] to give breath to **the image** of the [sea] beast, so that the image of the beast would even **speak and cause** as many as do not **worship the image** of the beast to be killed. [16] And he [the Image] causes all, the small and the great, and the rich and the poor, and the free men and the slaves, to be*

---

[1] Matthew 11:25; Revelation 2:7, 11, 17, 29; 3:6, 13, 22.

given **a mark** on their right hand or on their forehead, *17* and he provides that no one will be able to buy or to sell, except the one who has the mark, either the name of the beast or the number of his name (Revelation 13:15– 17).

Make no mistake. The final crisis is about *worship:* the true God versus Satan (through the Beast).[1]

*9 Then another angel, a third one, followed them, saying with a loud voice, "If anyone **worships** [reverence (outward show of respect or admiration); submits to; obeys] the beast and his image, and receives **a mark** on his forehead or on his hand, 10 he also will drink of the wine of the wrath of God (Revelation 14:9, 10).*

While there is plenty to dread about the Beast, thankfully there is an antidote against receiving its Mark: The Seal of the living God.

*2 Then I saw another angel ascending from the east, having **the seal of the living God.** And he cried with a loud voice to the four angels to whom it was granted to harm the earth and the sea, 3 saying, "Do not harm the earth, the sea, or the trees till we have **sealed** the servants of our God on their foreheads" (Revelation 7:2, 3 NKJV).*

Revelation confirms only two kingdoms at the end. Those who are *in* Christ and refuse to conform to the world have the safety of the Seal of God; those who have aligned themselves with the world system of government, at the expense of God, will receive the Mark of the Beast and will not have God's pro-

---

[1] Worship does not have to mean praying and singing. Worship involves loyalty and/or obedience.

tection against it. See Revelation 9:4. It is impossible to avoid the Mark of the Beast unless we are in the kingdom of God with our passport stamped with His official Seal. So, what is this Seal?

After the resurrection, when Jesus was about to return to heaven, He renewed an ancient promise to the disciples that God the Father would transform them by giving them a new Spirit. His instruction was to wait for what the Father had promised, which He explained would clothe them with power from on high. He made clear that power would be the result of the holy Spirit coming upon them.[1]

> [49] *And behold, I am sending forth* **the promise of My Father** *upon you; but you are to stay in the city until you are clothed with power from on high (Luke 24:49).*

> [4] *Gathering them together, He commanded them not to leave Jerusalem, but to wait for what the Father had promised, "Which," He said, "you heard of from Me. . . .* [8] *But you will receive power when the Holy Spirit has come upon you; and you shall be My witnesses . . . even to the remotest part of the earth" (Acts 1:4, 8).*

Recall that it was at Pentecost when the glorified Jesus "received from the Father the promise of the Holy Spirit" (Acts 2:33) and poured it out on His waiting disciples, filling them with miraculous power. This was the Old Testament promise fulfilled and was demonstrated in the miracles they performed, in their new boldness for Jesus, in the thousands of souls saved, and in their own transformed lives.[2]

The promise of the Spirit is in the new birth: Being born again by faith in Christ, you are *"sealed in Him with the Holy Spirit of promise,* who is given as a pledge of our inheritance"

---

[1] Ezekiel 11:19; 36:26; Jeremiah 24:7.
[2] Acts 5:14–16; 19:11, 12.

(Ephesians 1:13, 14). The Seal of the holy Spirit is our "down payment" for heaven from the day of our new birth-day until we are redeemed. The Spirit life of Jesus within us is the promise of the holy Spirit, the Seal of the living God![1]

> [22] *Who also sealed us and gave us the Spirit in our hearts as a pledge (2 Corinthians 1:22).*

> [14] *In order that **in** Christ Jesus the blessing of Abraham might come to the Gentiles, **so that we would receive the promise of the Spirit** through faith (Galatians 3:14).*

It appears, though, there is a second, special anointing of the Spirit for those who live through the final showdown against the dreaded Beast system. Revelation refers to this special group as the 144,000. This additional anointing of the Spirit, often referred to as the latter rain, is specifically reserved for this time and this group, as the final body of Christ. It is to equip the saints with the power they need to go through a time of trouble such has never been witnessed on the earth.[2]

> [1] *After this I saw four angels standing at the four corners of the earth, holding back the four winds of the earth so that no wind would blow on the earth, or on the sea, or on any tree.* [2] *And I saw another angel ascending from the rising of the sun, having the seal of the living God; and he cried out with a loud voice to the four angels to whom it was granted to harm the earth and the sea,* [3] *saying, "Do not harm the earth, or the sea, or the trees until we have sealed the bond-servants of our God on their foreheads."* [4] *And I heard **the number of***

---

[1] Revelation 15:2; 6:9; 20:4.
[2] Revelation 7:3, 4; 14:1; Daniel 12:1; Matthew 24:21; Mark 13:19.

***those who were sealed, one hundred and forty-
four thousand,*** *sealed from every tribe of the sons of
Israel (Revelation 7:1–4).*

*¹ Then I looked, and behold, the Lamb was standing on
Mount Zion, and with Him* **one hundred and forty-
four thousand,** *having His name and the name of His
Father written on their foreheads. ³ And they sang a
new song before the throne and before the four living
creatures and the elders; and no one could learn the
song except the one hundred and forty-four thousand
who had been purchased from the earth. ⁴ These are the
ones who have not been defiled with women, for they
have kept themselves chaste. These are the ones who
follow the Lamb wherever He goes. These have been
purchased from among men as first fruits to God and to
the Lamb. ⁵ And no lie was found in their mouth; they
are blameless (Revelation 14:1, 3–5).*

Again, we must translate the symbols. The 144,000 are
not physical Jews, but the spiritual seed of Abraham who
make up the new covenant church. Believers are sealed in
their forehead—and only in the forehead (mind/belief) because there is no such thing as being saved through works,
versus unbelievers who receive the Mark of the Beast in their
forehead or in their right hand (favor through outward com-
pliance). What is the evidence that we have the Seal of God?[1]

*³⁵ By this all men will know that you are My disciples, if
you have love for one another (John 13:35).*

¹⁴ We know that we have passed from death to life, be-

---

[1] Galatians 3:7, 8, 29; 6:16 (church = spiritual Israel); Romans 2:28, 29;
9:6-8; Philippians 3:3; 1Peter 2:9.

cause we love our brothers. The one who does not love re-mains in death (1 John 3:14).

²⁰ *If anyone says, "I love God," but hates his brother, he is a liar. For anyone who does not love his brother, whom he has seen, cannot love God, whom he has not seen (1 John 4:20).*

⁵ *Not as a new commandment to you, but one we have had from the beginning—that we love one another (2 John 1:5 BSB).*

They will know us by our love, not just love for the unlovely, but genuine love for those closest—our fellow brothers and sisters in Christ. We need not fear the Mark or the Antichrist, because the Father's name (Spirit/character) is written in our foreheads, and, if we remain faithful, we may have the privilege to receive this second anointing of Spirit power and represent God during the great test of the ages.[1]

As long as we do not *grieve* or *quench* the Spirit our soul will remain "sealed for the day of redemption" (Ephesians 4:30; 1 Thessalonians 5:19). Plus, we have the added promise that "God has given us eternal life, and this life is in His Son (1 John 5:11).[2]

True believers do not have the spirit of fear for what's coming, no matter what happens to us physically. We know the Father has *sealed* us in Christ and Christ is alive in us—and who can stand against Jesus Christ, the Son of the living God? Who can stand against the kingdom of God on earth?[3]

---

[1] KJV: Joel 2:23, 28–32; Zechariah 10:1; Hosea 6:3; Job 29:23; James 5:7.
[2] Isaiah 45:8; Deuteronomy 32:2; Hosea 10:12.
[3] Romans 8:31; Hebrews 13:6; 2 Kings 6:16; Isaiah 41:10.

[18] *Upon this rock [that Jesus is the Christ, the Son of the living God (see verse 16)] I will build My church; and the gates of Hades will not overpower it (Matthew 16:18).*

15

Deeper Answers, Questions, and Objections

Hard as it is to fathom, some who identify as Christian actually object to the idea of Jesus living His perfect life in us. Despite the focus of the New Testament on the crucial need for Christ to abide in us, and us in Him, a number of objections have been raised.

Is It Christ in You or *God the Holy Spirit?*

Most objections to Jesus being the One who lives in us go back to the concept of *God the Holy Spirit*. Many believe it is not actually Jesus Himself who now takes us through the struggles of life, but a third party. They say the cross gave us the fresh start we need by wiping our sins clean and relieving our guilt and that the life of Jesus then serves as our example of how we are to keep that record clear, with *God the Holy Spirit* being the one convicting us and guiding us to stay on the straight and narrow way.

Let's clarify that Holy Spirit is not a name. Holy is an adjective that describes the kind of spirit. Evil is another adjective that describes a different type of spirit. Spirit (noun) is defined as "wind, breath, spirit" [Strong's Concordance, G4151] and can be used with or without an adjective.[1]

Only one Man in human history has ever lived a sinless life since the day Adam ate of the forbidden tree. It took the Son of God to defeat sin and the Devil—and they expect us to do it in this broken, though *inspired,* human life? Impossible! The divine-human Spirit of Jesus is the only Superpower that could ever vanquish such a foe!

Really? Trying to *copy* the holy life of Jesus is not wise. Did anyone ever obtain Adam's life by *copying* it? Obviously, we had nothing to do with our physical existence because we've all inherited life from our parents, clearly without any input from us. We're here, and all we do is accept it. The same is equally true of our spiritual life. We cannot achieve a holy life by trying to copy the holiness of Jesus. We can only accept the born-again life He has given to us, how He has given it to us.

This concept of a third divine being seems largely rooted in the Comforter that Jesus taught the disciples His Father would send after His return to heaven.

> [16] *And I will pray the Father, and he shall give you another Comforter, that* **he** *may abide with you* **for ever** *(John 14:16 KJV).*

Because Jesus used third person pronouns—"He" as opposed to "I"—many take this as evidence of a separate divine person and build an entire doctrine on it. Yet, if we will keep

---

[1] Mark 1:26; 9:25; Acts 8:39; 17:16; Hebrews 12:23; 1 John 4:1.

an open mind and hear the Word of God, instead of the traditions of men, we don't have to be confused.[1]

Many focus on the word "another" and conclude it must be someone else, and miss the point of the passage. Note that the word "another" can be used in different ways. For example, you can either ask for "another" glass of water—more water in the same glass, or you can ask for "another" glass of water—water in a different glass. So, was Jesus telling the disciples about another (different) person to fill His role, or was He telling them about the same Person—Himself—filling another (different) role? Jesus Himself continued:

> [17] *That is the Spirit of truth, whom the world cannot receive, because it does not see Him or know Him, but* **you know Him** *because* **He abides with you** *and will be* **in** *you.* [18] **I will** *not leave you as orphans;* **I will come to you.** [19] *After a little while the world will no longer see Me, but* **you will see Me** *(John 14:17–19).*

Jesus comforts His friends and tells them plainly they already know who the Comforter is—the One who was living with them at that time would soon be in them. Specifically, *He* would come to them.

Next, a closer look at the ministry of Jesus makes it evident that He often spoke of Himself in the third person.[2]

> [38] *For whoever is ashamed of* **Me** *and* **My** *words in this adulterous and sinful generation, the* **Son of Man** *will also be ashamed of him when* **He** *comes in the glory of* **His** *Father with the holy angels (Mark 8:38).*

In this instance, Jesus refers to Himself in the first person in the present and in the third person in the future, all in one

---

[1] 2 Timothy 2:15; Proverbs 25:2; Deuteronomy 29:29.
[2] Mark 2:10, 28; 8:31; 9:9, 12; 10:33, 45, etc.

sentence. He even prayed to His Father in the third person.

> *3 This is eternal life, that they may know You, the only true God, and **Jesus Christ** whom You have sent (John 17:3).*

Notice that Jesus referred to only two divine Beings: God the Father and Himself, and that knowing *both* is eternal life. More importantly, He identified His Father as *the only true God*—He didn't even include Himself! It's a huge relief to know that God has not left us in doubt, but has given us the exact identity of the Comforter.

> *1 My little children, I am writing these things to you so that you may not sin. And if anyone sins, we have an **Advocate** with the Father, **Jesus Christ the righteous** (1 John 2:1).*

The same Greek word, *paraklétos,* was translated as Comforter in John chapters 14–16 and as Advocate in 1John 2 in the popular King James Version. The Author, John, used one Greek word in these passages, but Bible translators translated it into different English words. Yet, the apostle John understood the *paraklétos* to be a Comforter and an Advocate—namely, "Jesus Christ the righteous." Many newer Bible translations, such as the NIV, now use the word *Advocate* in John 14:16, instead of the word *Comforter.* Naturally, Jesus as the Son of Man is our Comforter and our Advocate, as well as our Intercessor. It only makes sense.

> *26 Now in the same way the Spirit also helps our weakness; for we do not know what to pray for as we should, but **the Spirit Himself intercedes for us** with groanings too deep for words; 27 and He who searches the hearts knows what the mind of the Spirit is, because*

He intercedes for the saints according to the will of God (Romans 8:26, 27).

Again, the Bible confirms exactly Who intercedes for us:

*34 Christ Jesus is He who died, yes, rather who was raised, who is at the right hand of God, who also **intercedes** for us. (Romans 8:34).*

The Scriptures could not be more explicit: It is *Christ in you.* His parting promise to His disciples was that He Himself would be with us until the very end of the world: *"I am with you always, even to the end of the age"* (Matthew 28:20). He says what He means and means what He says.

It was only Jesus Who left the glory of heaven to become a member of the human race, taking on our infirmities and defeating the Devil on his own turf. Enduring temptations and hardship, He submitted His personal will to the will of His Father all the way to the grave. All that agony and suffering would serve no purpose now if another deity entirely, one who had no personal experience whatsoever in the trials of humanity, was sent to help us overcome the trials of humanity, all while the One who has exactly the right experience is reassigned to the courts of heaven. Surely God is a better Commander than that![1]

15 For we do not have a high priest who cannot sympathize with our weaknesses, but One who has been tempted in all things as we are, yet without sin (Hebrews 4:15).

Remember, we are the temple, and only a human priest can rightfully enter the temple. The Messiah came to earth to accomplish a very specific mission. If just anyone, no matter

---

[1] Matthew 26:36–27:54; Luke 22:42; Hebrews 5:7–9.

how holy, could fill that role, the Father would not have given His own Son so needlessly.

If we are to take the Bible for what it says, believing it without molding God into an image of our own making, then we must be willing to admit there is no third deity, no middleman between us and our heavenly Father other than Jesus, the only begotten Son of the only true God. From His own mouth, He is our only Way to the Father! See John 14:6. There is no other!

No—there are not two Mediators. The Bible is crystal clear: There is only *one* Mediator, or Intercessor, between man and God.

> *5 For there is one God and **one Mediator** also between God and men, **the man Christ Jesus,** 6 who gave Himself as a ransom for all, the testimony given at the proper time (1 Timothy 2:5, 6).*

As our *divine-human* Mediator, Christ is the *only* connecting link between the *divine* Father and the *human* race. Don't be afraid of the Truth.

> *3 Seeing that His divine power has granted to us everything pertaining to life and godliness, through the **true knowledge** of Him who called us by His own glory and excellence (2 Peter 1:3).*

How wonderfully tremendous is this salvation we've been given, greater than any mortal mind could imagine![1]

Via Christ in You or Obeying the Law?

Another common objection to *Christ in you* usually has to do with the false idea that the Ten Commandments have been

---

[1] 2 Peter 1:16; 1 Corinthians 2:4, 5.

done away with. Christians, in general, agree that the ceremonial laws and ordinances were "nailed to the cross," but some insist the Commandments are to remain front and center of the Christian's everyday life. See Colossians 2:14.

These cannot let go of the belief that *they* need to contribute to their salvation. It's as if Jesus Himself is not enough to save them; they must help Jesus save them. That usually involves a laundry list of good deeds and habits they feel would gain God's favor, along with their personal resolve to resist temptation and sin. The problem with this is focus. Without realizing it, their Christianity comes down to "salvation by works" or "salvation by knowledge". They believe as they gain more knowledge from the Bible, they can overcome sin by *choosing* to live out that knowledge through sheer willpower and self-control.

How amazing, considering it was this very attitude that got us in this mess in the first place. Satan tempted Eve with "the knowledge of good and evil," implying that they needed only knowledge and information to be good—not God. Ironically, these folks have no problem believing we can be possessed by evil spirits, but not by God's Spirit. They call it spiritualism or New Age. This actually credits more power to the Devil than to the divine Father and Son! It also forces us to deny the plain teachings of the Bible.

*[27] To whom God willed to make known what is the riches of the glory of this mystery among the Gentiles, which is **Christ in you**, the hope of glory (Colossians 1:27).*

*[5] Test yourselves to see if you are in the faith; examine yourselves! Or do you not recognize this about yourselves, that **Jesus Christ is in you**—unless indeed you fail the test? (2 Corinthians 13:5).*

How can we deny that Jesus Christ Himself must live in us? Otherwise, we fail! The Amplified Bible adds we would be rejected as counterfeit!

Their notion of how the gospel works is that Jesus gives us inspiration. That is, by studying and admiring the life and ministry of Jesus it will inspire us to do as He did. We then must imitate His life, doing as much as we can for as long as we can. When temptation closes in and we start to become weak, we are to turn to Jesus for help before we fall. That's when He swoops in with encouragement and boosts our morale. It's like the old saying, "The Lord helps those who help themselves." Another popular saying is, "When I am weak, He is strong."

Seriously? These are old proverbs, not Bible. We are *always* weak in our own power, and we are never strong enough to battle against a super-human villain like Satan, much less our own corrupt hearts. Or don't they recall Jesus's words, "Apart from Me you can do nothing"? (John 15:5).

Under their scenario, where is the actual help? Unless they assume this verse to mean, "Apart from My pep talks you can do nothing." Or, maybe it means, "Apart from My infallible advice you can to nothing." This leaves us to be righteous in our own power. Anyone who has attempted this knows full well how exhausting it can be to try to live perfectly through our own willpower, all day, every day. Even a simple resolution to "be good" is a setup to fail. One stressful traffic jam, one big argument with our spouse, and—oops, it's back to square one.

Under no circumstances are we fallen mortals ever strong enough to do *anything* on our own to contribute to our salvation. This is what the grace of God is all about.

> [8] *For by grace you have been saved through faith; and that not of yourselves, it is the gift of God (Ephesians 2:8).*

⁹ *And He has said to me, "My grace is sufficient for you, for power is perfected in weakness." Most gladly, therefore, I will rather boast about my weaknesses, so that the* **power of Christ** *may dwell* **in** *me (2 Corinthians 12:9).*

Salvation is a gift, not a career. In digital terms, think of it as a paywall that Jesus paid for us with His life—and He's the Paywall! We subscribe to Jesus, then we get all the benefits of what's behind the Paywall. So, chasing after righteousness is not our business; it's a benefit provided to those behind the Paywall. Our job is to choose the Paywall. We choose Christ and the rest is on Him. His job isn't just counsel or inspiration or even a perfect example. It's His strength, His power, His victorious life—Him! We are "made perfect in weakness" only in Him. This applies every moment of every day. Always. Without. Fail. Then, and only then, can we "do all things *through Him* who strengthens" us (Philippians 4:13). A better version of those old proverbs would be, "The Lord helps those who trust in Him" and "I am always weak, but He is always strong."

The real issue with the law is not whether it's been eliminated; it's that no one is able to keep it. Rather than doing away with the law, it's a matter of putting it in its proper place. The purpose of the law is to expose the fact that we have a sin problem and have no power to fix it. Similarly, a speed limit sign is the written law displayed to make the speeder aware that he is driving outside the law, but it has no power to put on the brakes for him. When we are converted, we give the driving over to Jesus, who always does right. Another analogy of the law is a mirror: It reflects what we can't see on our own— the dirt on our face. Yet, a mirror can't clean us up. So, too, the law of God can only make us aware of our need of Jesus.

⁸ We know that the law is good if one uses it properly.

⁹ We also know that the law is made not for the right-eous but for lawbreakers and rebels, the ungodly and sinful, the unholy and irreligious, for those who kill their fathers or mothers, for murderers, ¹⁰ for the sexu-ally immoral, for those practicing homosexuality, for slave traders [human traffickers] and liars and perjur-ers—and for whatever else is contrary to the sound doc-trine (1 Timothy 1:8–10 NIV).

The law was made for the lawless, those who are outside of Christ, who commit everything from lying to adultery to murder—all the things that flow from a sin nature. This ex-cludes no one. And, yes, we were all born that way. That's why Jesus said we must be born again![1]

²¹ Is there a conflict, then, between God's law and God's promises? Absolutely not! **If the law could give us new life, we could be made right with God by obeying it.** *²² But the Scriptures declare that* **we are all prisoners of sin,** *so we receive God's promise of freedom only by believing in Jesus Christ. ²³* **Before the way of faith in Christ** *was available to us, we were placed under guard by the law. We were kept in protective custody, so to speak, until the way of faith was revealed. ²⁴ Let me put it another way. The law was our guardian until Christ came; it protected us until we could be made right with God through faith. ²⁵ And now that the way of faith has come, we no longer need the law as our guardian. ²⁶ For you are all children of God through faith in Christ Jesus (Galatians 3:21–26 NLT).*

---

[1] 1 Corinthians 6:9, 10; Galatians 5:19–21; Romans 1:21–32.

Before we had faith in Jesus, the law was our teacher instructing us on the standard for living a moral life, while at the same time exposing our inability to perform it. The law exposes the fact that humans are not good in themselves and cannot do good. Thus, it made sin appear more sinful in order to teach us our need for a Savior so we would accept Him.

Once we accept Jesus, though, we no longer need to be directed to Him. Compare it to a road trip. There are signs along the way to indicate how many miles to the destination, with the last sign at the border welcoming visitors. Once there, however, there are no signs directing you to where you already are. Remember, Jesus is our righteousness and the law was not made for a righteous Man. Once we're in the Man Jesus, we are in His righteousness; we have arrived. The commandments, then, have done their job and we no longer need this mirror, this road sign.

For context, in the *old covenant,* God appointed a series of laws, including the ten commandments, later called "the ministry of death, in letters engraved on stones" (2 Corinthians 3:7) to teach of the *law of consequences.* The ancient Jews were given 600-plus external rules for right versus wrong, covering every facet of life. It was a system of *shadows*—allegories or symbols—that pointed to and illustrated the work of the future Messiah. It was not spiritual reality and was never intended as a means of salvation. Punishment for breaking these laws seemed harsh but taught the ultimate consequence of rejecting the Messiah.[1]

Being "under the law," the children of Israel were to exercise faith in the promises of God as they performed the sacrifices and rituals that symbolized the true Lamb of God to come. So, yes, salvation was available in Old Testament times, and still by faith, but based upon the *promises* of the future events surrounding the cross.[2]

---

[1] Romans 3:20; 7:7–13.
[2] Hebrews 10:1; 11:39, 40; Hebrews 8:13; 12:24.

[18] For if the inheritance could be received by keeping the law, then it would not be the result of accepting God's promise. But God graciously gave it to Abraham as a promise. [19] Why, then, was the law given? **It was given alongside the promise to show people their sins.** *But the law was designed to last only until the coming of the child [Jesus] who was promised. God gave his law through angels to Moses, who was the mediator between God and the people (Galatians 3:18, 19 NLT).*

God's original covenant to Abraham was that his lineage would produce the long-awaited Messiah. After Sarah failed to conceive, Abraham fathered a child with Sarah's maid Hagar. Hagar gave birth through Abraham's own efforts. But God said that only Sarah would produce his son. Later, Sarah, well past the time of child-bearing, gave birth through a miracle of God.[1]

Four hundred years later, God *added* the law in order to restrain sin, and as a guide for morality and worship, *"until the coming of the child."* See Galatians 3:15–18. *It did not alter or add to the original promise to Abraham.* When the appointed time came, Jesus Christ established a *new covenant* based upon a better system: *He* was the promise given to father Abraham! With Jesus, the old covenant of rules and rituals meant to restrain sin and teach about the Messiah was no longer needed. The new covenant of the Spirit working within was established.

[6] He has enabled us to be ministers of his new covenant. **This is a covenant not of written laws, but of the Spirit.** *The old written covenant ends in* **death;** *but under the new covenant, the Spirit gives life (2 Corinthians 3:6 NLT).*

---

[1] Genesis 16–21; Hebrews 11:11.

Hagar is a symbol of the old covenant—Mt. Sinai/law], and Sarah is a symbol of the new covenant—faith in Jesus. It may shock us to realize what the apostle Paul instructs us to do:

> [21] *Tell me, you who want to be under law, do you not listen to the law?* [22] *For it is written that Abraham had two sons, one by the bondwoman and one by the free woman.* [23] *But the son by the bondwoman was born according to the flesh, and the son by the free woman through the promise.* [24] *This is allegorically speaking, for these women are two covenants: one proceeding from Mount Sinai bearing children who are to be slaves; she is Hagar.* [25] *Now this Hagar is Mount Sinai in Arabia and corresponds to the present Jerusalem, for she is in slavery with her children.* [28] *And you brethren, like Isaac, are children of promise.* [29] *But as at that time he who was born according to the flesh persecuted him who was born according to the Spirit, so it is now also.* [30] *But what does the Scripture say?* "CAST OUT THE BONDWOMAN AND HER SON, FOR THE SON OF THE BONDWOMAN SHALL NOT BE AN HEIR WITH THE SON OF THE FREE WOMAN."* [31] *So then, brethren, we are not children of a bondwoman, but of the free woman (Galatians 4:21–25, 28–31).*

We are to "cast out the bondwoman and her son"! The slave Hagar represents Mt. Sinai, that is, the law; her son represents the works of the law. We're told to drive out the law and works, because they persecute the born-again believer. Two reminders: (1) The law only makes us aware of sin; it has no power to transform us; and, (2) Power is a Person. Since being born-again, we are now bonded with the one Person who has the power to free us from the ministration of the law of sin and death. Yet, the commandments are still valid to point other lawless ones to Christ. So, yes, the commandment is still holy and just and good.

We're all born in an old covenant condition with the law as our standard for what's good and right. When we accept Jesus, we are born again in the new covenant of His indwelling Spirit—He becomes our standard. Do we not realize that if we continue to order our lives by law-keeping, we are no better than slaves (Hagar)? That following after the law leaves us under the old covenant of the flesh, as servants, and not in the Spirit of Christ as adopted sons and daughters? Being "severed from Christ" and "fallen from grace" (Galatians 5:4), Christ is of no benefit to us.

Sadly, those who continue to live by the law cannot also live in Christ. In the end they will profess to have *worked* wonderfully in His name, but in reality, it is works without relationship. Sadly, His answer will sting their souls: "I never knew you; DEPART FROM ME, YOU WHO PRACTICE LAWLESSNESS" (Matthew 7:23). All their so-called good deeds will be counted as lawlessness.

> *¹ Now I say, as long as the heir is a child, he does not differ at all from a slave although he is owner of everything, ² but he is under guardians and managers until the date set by the father. ³ So also we, while we were children, were held in bondage under the elemental things of the world. ⁴ But when the fullness of the time came, **God sent forth His Son,** born of a woman, born under the Law, ⁵ so that He might redeem those who were under the Law, that we might receive the adoption as sons. ⁶ Because you are sons, **God has sent forth the Spirit of His Son into our hearts, crying, "Abba! Father!"** ⁷ Therefore you are no longer a slave, but a son; and if a son, then an heir through God (Galatians 4:1–7).*

With the Spirit of Jesus in us, our new hearts cry out to God: *Daddy! Father!* God sent forth His Son from heaven the first time to be born of Mary, in the flesh and under the law. At Pentecost, God sent forth His Son again, this time in the Spirit and directly into our hearts. With Christ in us, we are no longer slaves, like children under an instructor, chastised into obeying "the letter" of legal rules. We have received the "law of the Spirit of life in Christ Jesus" (Romans 8:2), and Jesus doesn't need laws to make us perfect. He is perfect. He is everything we need for salvation.

> *18 But if you are led by the Spirit, you are not under the Law (Galatians 5:18).*

If we can see the truth that Jesus Christ is living His life through us, why are we concerned about obeying the law? Did Jesus ever break the law? Of course not. Christ is our Righteousness, and there is no law against righteousness. When we partake of His divine nature, living a moral life as outlined in the law will be a natural consequence. Christ in us will do far above what the law requires. He will fill us with a heart of Love.

> *36 "Teacher, which is the great commandment in the Law?" 37 And He said to him, "'YOU SHALL LOVE THE LORD YOUR GOD WITH ALL YOUR HEART, AND WITH ALL YOUR SOUL, AND WITH ALL YOUR MIND.' 38 This is the great and foremost commandment. 39 The second is like it, 'YOU SHALL LOVE YOUR NEIGHBOR AS YOURSELF.'" 40 Upon these two commandments depend the whole Law and the Prophets (Matthew 22:36–40).*

> *14 For the whole Law is fulfilled in one word, in the statement, "YOU SHALL LOVE YOUR NEIGHBOR AS YOURSELF" (Galatians 5:14).*

Since God is love, and Jesus is love, we will rise far above just keeping a set of legal rules. The Love in us is not self-seeking, and doesn't keep track of any wrong done to it. Love doesn't repay evil, but "overcome[s] evil with good" (Romans 12:21). True love doesn't look for a return on investment—what we can get out of it. True love just loves. It gives.

> *4 Love is patient, love is kind. It does not envy, it does not boast, it is not proud. 5 It is not rude, it is not self-seeking, it is not easily angered, it keeps no account of wrongs. 6 Love takes no pleasure in evil, but rejoices in the truth. 7 It bears all things, believes all things, hopes all things, endures all things. 8 Love never fails (1 Corinthians 13:4–8).*

> *5 The love of God has been poured out within our hearts through the Holy Spirit who was given to us (Romans 5:5).*

With this gift of Love in us, we won't have to bite our tongue to keep from speaking our mind, because our mind is His, patient and kind. We will have a pure heart, so we won't have to wrestle to resist lust. More than loving our enemies, we won't see them as enemies but as children of God in need of a revelation of Jesus; we will see them for who they are, prodigal sons and daughters—even if they don't know it—and we will remember how much their Father longs for them to come home. We won't have a legalistic mindset toward them as did the older brother. Rather, we will accept even the most deplorable as identical in worth because we know we all start as prodigals, and we are all equally loved.

Our consistent goal should be to seek Love—that is, God the Father and His Son. There should be no other person, no other belief or doctrine, no law or commandment, to distract us from that focus. But if all else fails, one typical complaint against these beautiful truths is the accusation that this is "cheap grace." Without apology, that is absolutely true. It is grace so cheap it's free!

> *¹⁵ But the **free gift** is not like the transgression. For if by the transgression of the one the many died, much more did the grace of God and the [free] gift by the grace of the one Man, Jesus Christ, abound to the many (Romans 5:15).*

The only cost to us is to give Him our lives.

How the Bible Defines Sin

Another argument against *Christ in you* involves the Bible's definition of sin.

> *⁴ Whosoever committeth sin transgresseth also the law: for sin is the transgression of the law (1 John 3:4 KJV).*

Some like to pinpoint this verse as the only biblical definition of sin. Therefore, sin cannot be our nature, but strictly our wrong behavior. While true on an outward level, this definition is sorely lacking. The word sin means "missing the mark"—but what mark? For example, showing partiality is a sin (see James 2:9), yet the commandments do not say "Thou shalt not show partiality." It is also a sin when you know to do good but don't. See James 4:17. In this case, not doing something is called sin. Obviously, the Bible has other definitions of sin apart from breaking the commandments. Being lawless, being partial, refusing to do good—these are examples of a life apart from Jesus. Jesus was the One who pointed out there's more to the commandments than ten *Thou shalt nots.*

*[21] You have heard that the ancients were told, 'YOU SHALL NOT COMMIT MURDER' and 'Whoever commits murder shall be liable to the court.'[22] But I say to you that everyone who is **angry** with his brother shall be guilty before the court (Matthew 5:21, 22).*

Most everyone agrees that murder is a grievous sin and a clear violation of the sixth commandment. But the commandment doesn't forbid anger. If sin is defined only as breaking the law, then Jesus could not have expanded our understanding of murder to include the hidden attitudes and negative emotions that give birth to such actions, whether or not there's intent to act on them. In this, He reveals our actions are only symptoms. Rather, the deeper issue is in the spirit of the person. This, again, is the carnal nature. In contrast, our nature transformed will reflect the heart of Jesus, and the heart of Jesus is love, always.

For another perspective, there are examples of what may seem to be Jesus condoning, encouraging, and even participating in breaking the law. Yet, we know Jesus never broke the law and never sinned. One familiar story is in John 8:3–5, of a woman taken in the act of adultery. The law commanded that the adulteress (and the adulterer[1]) be put to death. Instead, Jesus forgave the woman and brilliantly exposed the hypocrisy of her accusers until they all abandoned their plot (verses 6–9).

We see then that the law served its intended purpose of exposing the sin of adultery. But the woman now stood face to face with the Savior she so desperately needed, so the law was no longer necessary—and stoning would not save her soul. The living Law of Love was present to do for her what the commandments never could—deliver her from the power of

---

[1] The man wasn't brought for public accusation as per the law. See Exodus 20:14; Leviticus 20:10.

sin: "Go and sin no more" (John 8:11 KJV). Jesus spoke a greater power into her life.

Another event demonstrates this further. Another woman had suffered from an issue of blood for twelve years and had battled her disease until she had exhausted her money without a cure. According to the law, she was unclean for those twelve years. This required her to be isolated from her family and friends because everything and everyone she touched also became unclean. In her desperation, she sought out the Messiah while He was in the midst of a throng. As she pressed through the crowd—touching many in the process—she willfully disregarded the law. With deliberate intent, she touched the hem of Jesus's garment.

Astonishingly, or not, Jesus did not rebuke her for this blatant disregard for the law, nor did He complain that He and the others were now unclean. Rather, she was rewarded with immediate healing and He praised her for her faith. Again, we see the law was irrelevant as this woman stood in the presence of the great Physician who cured her body and soul.[1]

Belief that the Omnipresent Spirit is Angels

An alarming number of people are accepting a belief that God Himself is not actually omnipresent, that is, He does not have the ability to be in all places at once through His personal Spirit. Instead, they believe God the Father, and especially Jesus Christ, are limited to Their physical location, currently in heaven, and that both the Father and Son are present throughout the universe only by way of the seemingly endless number of angels who carry Their will and Their blessings throughout all creation.

We'll try to ignore the fact that at first glance this doctrine

---

[1] Luke 8:43–48; Leviticus 15:19–27.

has attempted the impossible by limiting the One being in the universe we are told is all-mighty.

> *⁷ Can you discover the depths of God? Can you discover the limits of the **Almighty?** (Job 11:7).*

This stems, in part, from a faulty interpretation of the Bible's reference to angels as ministering spirits.

> *¹³ But to which of the angels has He ever said, "SIT AT MY RIGHT HAND, UNTIL I MAKE YOUR ENEMIES A FOOTSTOOL FOR YOUR FEET"? ¹⁴ Are they not all ministering spirits, sent out **to render service** for the sake of those who will inherit salvation? (Hebrews 1:13, 14).*

The first question is, So, what happens in those places where an angel is not physically present? We must conclude that the avenue for God and His goodness would be absent from that place.

> *²⁷ The spirit of man is the lamp of the LORD, searching all the innermost parts of his being (Proverbs 20:27).*

> *²² The Lord be with your spirit (2 Timothy 4:22).*

Being made in the image of God, mankind also has a spirit just as God does. There are times when people minister to other people, so we too can be considered ministering spirits.

> *¹⁴ And my trial which was in my flesh you did not despise or reject, **but you received me as an angel of God,** even as Christ Jesus (Galatians 4:14 NKJV).*

Does that make us the holy Spirit? If it were true, that neither God Almighty nor Jesus Christ is omnipresent, the angels would be responsible for everything the Bible attributes to the holy Spirit of God. It's the Spirit that abides *in* our hearts, fills us with the fruits of righteousness, convicts us of sin, guides us into all truth, and empowers us with spiritual gifts, and much more. Some have suggested as many as seventy different functions of the holy Spirit.[1]

In other words, our salvation would be credited to *angels,* created beings capable of falling into sin just like Lucifer! Our born-again experience would be the result of *angels* renewing us with their own life, not Jesus. This is blasphemy, attributing to created beings what alone belongs to God! While we may not all be familiar with this idea, it is not new. Paul warned of something similar in his own day.

> [18] *Let no one keep defrauding you of your prize by delighting in self-abasement and* **the worship of the angels,** *taking his stand on visions he has seen, inflated without cause by his fleshly mind (Colossians 2:18).*

Ascribing to angels the work of God's holy Spirit is angel worship. Yes, angels are ministering spirits, but there is a great difference between the angels who "render service" or aid versus actually *accomplishing* man's transformation and salvation, which alone is the work of God.

Angels have been involved in the mission to save mankind *since the beginning.* The first recorded example is an angel with a flaming sword who guarded the Tree of Life once Adam and Eve had been removed from the Garden. See Genesis 3:24. Two angels were sent to Sodom to deliver Lot and his family prior to its destruction. See Genesis 19:1–26. And in Genesis 28:12, Jacob was given a dream representing the *steady involvement* of angels in the affairs of man, symbol-

---

[1] John 14:17; 1 Corinthians 6:19, 20; Romans 8:9; John 16:7–11, 13; 1 Corinthians 12:7–11.

ized as they traveled up and down a staircase that connected heaven to earth. Jesus Himself said He is the staircase the angels are "ascending and descending" upon, showing it is through Him that the angels work—not vice versa—and His reach is from heaven to earth (John 1:51).

Why is this important? Jesus made an interesting statement about the work of the Spirit:

> *[38] He who believes in Me, as the Scripture said, 'From his innermost being will flow rivers of living water.' [39] But this He spoke of the Spirit, whom those who believed in Him* **were to receive; for the Spirit was not yet given, because Jesus was not yet glorified** *(John 7:38, 39).*

While the Spirit has existed as long as God has existed, the *indwelling* Spirit was a future work of the Messiah. Angels have been involved in aiding mankind since Eden, but the divine-human Spirit that Jesus referred to didn't exist and couldn't be given until He was perfected and glorified, because *He* is that perfect, glorified Spirit! See Hebrews 5:8, 9.

We recognize that event, when the Spirit was given, as Pentecost, not when angels were "poured out" in power, but when the triumphant Savior Himself returned to fill His waiting disciples with His own victorious life and power!

> *[31] "Therefore I say to you, any sin and blasphemy shall be forgiven people, but blasphemy against the Spirit shall not be forgiven. [32] Whoever speaks a word against the Son of Man, it shall be forgiven him; but whoever speaks against the Holy Spirit, it shall not be forgiven him, either in this age or in the age to come (Matthew 12:31, 32).*

Blasphemy against the Son of God will be forgiven but not blasphemy against angels? This passage shows the absurdity of believing angels are the holy Spirit.

Where's the Evidence?

Still others are skeptical of Christ literally (in Spirit) living in us because they cannot see the evidence of supernatural power in their own life or in the lives of other professed believers. They ask how anyone could be born-again and partake of the divine nature, possess the holy life of God's own Son, and still make mistakes and have faults.

We need to start by separating those who are truly born-again and love the Lord but still experience faults from those who claim to be Christians but love the world. Next, 1 John 5:17 says, "All unrighteousness is sin: and there is a sin not leading to death." Incredible as it may be for our law-oriented minds to grasp, there is a type of sin that does not lead to death.[1]

As we walk in "the Way" of the life of Jesus, our memories and habits play an active role in how we deal with the challenges of daily life. While our spirit has been renewed in the new birth, our mind tends to work in certain patterns due to a lifetime of those memories and habits, which can hinder our faith. Thus, our failings can often be summed up in Christ's repeated rebuke, "You of little faith." See Matthew 6:30; 14:31.

[25] *If we live by the Spirit, let us also walk by the Spirit (Galatians 5:25).*

According to the apostle Paul, walking by or in the Spirit is more than living in the Spirit. On those days when we are not fully focused on Jesus, we may "miss the mark" of abiding in Christ. Yet, this stumbling is not unto death, no more than

---

[1] Luke 6:43, 44; 1 John 5:16.

Peter was left to drown when he took his eyes off Jesus when walking on the water. See Matthew 14:25–32. Like Peter, despite our lack, we still have faith in Christ and are still in the Way of salvation, and Jesus will answer our call for help. Similarly, when a husband and wife are emotionally distant, it may affect their fellowship, but it doesn't affect their relationship: They are still married. If they continue to ignore intimacy then, yes, it can lead to a broken relationship. Likewise, our relationship with the Father and Son will not break until we stop abiding in Jesus and walk away.

The good news is God wants to help us avoid these times of stumbling and He is willing to use His divine superpower to make that happen. He has told us what we need: a vital connection of trust in Him through His Son; to spend personal time with Him daily, in prayer and the Word, singing to and talking with Him, and listening; to abandon our cares to Him.

He wants us to know *Him* as a Person, not just know *about* Him. He wants to share His heart of love. This transforming walk will equip us to face each day. As our focus changes, those pesky memories and habits will fade. As we keep our eyes on Jesus, we won't have a roller coaster ride of good days and bad days—not that we won't have bad days; we just won't be identified by them.

Expect that some of those bad days will be solely because we belong to Christ and not the world. We were called to suffer for Jesus for doing good. But let us never allow our suffering to change our doing good. If our motive is pure, if our motive is love, nothing can shake us. Every day will be blessed knowing He is always here, always Sovereign, always Love, despite whatever the "winds and waves" of life hurl at us. So, the moral of the story is, if you want to miraculously walk on water through the storms of life, don't take your eyes off Jesus![1]

---

[1] 2 Timothy 3:12; John 15:20.

The time is soon coming when God will cleanse our temple-mind of the memories of past sins and failures. Until then, we must be transformed daily by allowing our minds to be renewed and brought into harmony with our renewed spirit in Christ.

> ² *And do not be conformed to this world, but be transformed by the renewing of your mind, so that you may prove what the will of God is, that which is good and acceptable and perfect (Romans 12:2).*

What About Babies?

Some have asked, If we are all born with a sin nature, what about babies who can't understand what sin is, with all its ramifications, but die before they are old enough to repent? The answer is, though all are born under Adam's curse, Christ "died for all" (2 Corinthians 5:15) and His grace covers all, from the Garden to the last baby ever born.

> ¹⁶ *For of His fullness we have **all** received, and grace upon grace (John 1:16).*

> ¹¹ *For the grace of God that brings salvation has appeared to all men (Titus 2:11 NKJV).*

The Lamb's Book of Life was written "since the foundation of the world" (Revelation 13:8; 17:8). Because God's promise concerning the mission of Jesus was so certain it would succeed, the names of every beneficiary of that mission were saved in a special book known as the Book of Life. Whether a literal book or not, every name of every human to ever live was considered saved before any were born. Through the abundant grace of God and the blood of the Lamb not yet slain, we were all recipients of His coming sacrifice, predestined to be saved. We just accept it by faith. Now, that's the true saving power of a Superhero![1]

> [4] *Just as He chose us in Him before the foundation of the world, that we would be holy and blameless before Him. In love* [5] *He predestined us to adoption as sons through Jesus Christ to Himself, according to the kind intention of His will,* [6] *to the praise of the glory of His grace, which He freely bestowed on us in the Beloved.* [7] *In Him we have redemption through His blood, the forgiveness of our trespasses, according to the riches of His grace (Ephesians 1:4–7).*

Babies are also written in the Lamb's Book of Life because they too are covered under the grace of Jesus that covers all. If and when they get old enough to become aware of their carnal nature, they too will need to accept Jesus and be born again.[2]

However, being predestined to be saved does not *guarantee* we will be saved, nor is it a matter of "once saved, always saved."

> [28] *May they be blotted out of the book of life and may they not be recorded with the righteous (Psalm 69:28).*

> [33] *Whoever has sinned against Me, I will blot him out of My book (Exodus 32:33).*

Even before creation, the whole world was reconciled to God by the cross of Jesus Christ—which was still future—and covered by His grace. Sadly, not everyone in the whole world will be saved because salvation is by faith in a personal Savior. We have to *believe* Him and *receive* Him individually, and

---

[1] 2 Timothy 1:9.
[2] This includes people with mental disabilities, without the capacity to understand sin. And just because someone dies tragically, doesn't mean they're lost eternally.

not everyone in the world will believe and receive this great gift.

> *17 For God did not send the Son into the world to judge the world, but that the world might be saved through Him. 18 He who believes in Him is not judged; he who does not believe has been judged **already,** because he has not believed in the name of the only begotten Son of God. 36 He who believes in the Son has eternal life (John 3:17, 18, 36).*

Remember, faith is pivotal in claiming all the blessings of God that are in Christ. Even many who believe today may not, for reasons unknown, still believe tomorrow. So, beware, we can have salvation in Christ now and still reject Him later.[1]

Understanding What Salvation Is

We need to recognize that our salvation does not hinge upon individual acts of obedience or disobedience. It's about whose life we are living—that is, who is in control of our life. Are we living a self-oriented life, independent of God, making decisions based upon our own limited knowledge and desires? Or are we living a Christ-centered life, recognizing how truly dependent we are upon Him, seeking His will for our lives above all else, and leaning on His perfect wisdom and sound judgment for even simple daily direction?

If we have the Son of God, we have eternal life. If we don't have the Son, we don't have eternal life. Either we have Him or we don't. This is salvation.

> *11 And the testimony is this, that God has given us eternal life, and this life is in His Son. 12 He who has the Son*

---

[1] 1 Timothy 4:1–4. In 1 Samuel 10:1–12, King Saul was filled with the Spirit of God and given a new heart. Later, in 1 Samuel 16:14, the Spirit departed the arrogant king because he consistently rejected God's word.

has the life; he who does not have the Son of God does not have the life (1 John 5:11, 12).

It can all be summed up this way:

24 *The God who made the world and everything in it is the Lord of heaven and earth and does not live in temples built by human hands.* 25 *And he is not served by human hands, as if he needed anything. Rather, he himself gives everyone life and breath and everything else.* 26 *From one man [Adam] he made all the nations, that they should inhabit the whole earth; and he marked out their appointed times in history and the boundaries of their lands.* 27 *God did this so that they would seek him and perhaps reach out for him and find him, though he is not far from any one of us.* 28 *'For in him we live and move and have our being....'* 29 *Therefore since we are God's offspring, we should not think that the divine being is like gold or silver or stone—an image made by human design and skill.* 30 *In the past God overlooked such ignorance, but now he commands all people everywhere to repent.* 31 *For he has set a day when he will judge the world with justice by the man [Jesus] he has appointed. He has given proof of this to everyone by raising him from the dead (Acts 17:24–31 NIV).*

16

The Threefold Mission of the One True Superhero

14 The secret of the LORD is for those who fear Him, and He will make them know His covenant (Psalm 25:14).

7 Surely the Lord GOD does nothing unless He reveals His secret counsel to His servants the prophets (Amos 3:7).

It is human nature to be afraid of what we don't understand. That's why it has always been in God's plan that His children understand what this Ultimate Universal War (UUW) is all about. When many of the hard questions about God are answered, when we understand the big picture from beginning to end, we will realize there's nothing to be afraid of: God's unconditional love for us compels Him to come to our rescue.

In order to see the big picture, we start with what we already know about the UUW beginning in heaven when Lucifer brought accusations against the character and government of Almighty God. But what specifically was it all about? We get clues when Satan confronted Eve in the Garden. By challenging what God said, Satan unmasked his intention to cast doubt on the honesty and integrity of God's character.

Comparing Ezekiel 28:12–19 and Isaiah 14:12–14, with these clues in Genesis and elsewhere in the Bible, and we can conclude that Satan introduced three crises for the universe: He cast serious doubt on the pure *character* of God (that God lied in order to selfishly withhold something good); he charged that the *government* of God (ruling from within through the Spirit) was faulty and inferior; and he succeeded in convincing Adam and Eve to join him in rejecting God's government in favor of self-government (infamously stated as "Do what thou wilt"). From this, we see the loss of the human race wasn't the only thing that went wrong, so saving humanity wasn't the only problem to solve.

God couldn't defend Himself by boasting about how awesome He is, even though it would all be true. Again, God needed a Witness, Someone who knew Him in a personal way to champion for Him on His behalf, while at the same time be able to fulfill the plan to save humanity. The Plan of Salvation that sent the Son of God to earth was a *three-fold mission* to reverse all the damage that Satan had caused in the universe. That three-fold mission can be summarized as: (1) to reveal God's true character; (2) to redeem humanity; and (3) to vindicate God's government.

Understanding this tri-mission of Jesus will help us see the perfect wisdom behind our salvation and know why Jesus—the only true Superhero—could alone qualify for this enormous job.

MISSION #1: Reveal the True Character of Almighty God

Since only divinity is good, then only divinity can reveal divinity. No created being could bring the full truth of God to others. Only Jesus, God's only begotten Son, could be that Champion.

Jesus Himself said: "No one has ever seen God. God's only Son, the one who is closest to the Father's heart, has made him known" (John 1:18 GWT). The apostle Paul further explained that it is through the Son that we can have "the Light of the knowledge of the *glory [revealed character] of God in the face of Christ"* (2 Corinthians 4:6).

> *[14] And the Word became flesh and dwelt among us, and we beheld His glory, the glory as of the only begotten of the Father, full of grace and truth (John 1:14 NKJV).*

Only the *Son of God* can reveal the true character and nature of the Father, because He alone has existed in the kind of intimate relationship that only a Father and Son can have. Plus, He shares the same nature. That's why Jesus could say, "He who has seen Me has seen the Father" (John 14:9).

The fact that Jesus had a Source in the Father and a beginning in eternity past, before the creation of anything, is key to how He could become a Man and walk among men. Born of God, and later born of Mary into the family of Adam, Jesus became the divine-human link between God and humanity. Only through Him have we been able to learn the truth about what God is really like.

In the final hours before the cross, Jesus prayed to the Father, proclaiming that His first mission—to reveal the truth about the character of God the Father—was complete.

> [4] ***I glorified You*** *on the earth* **having accomplished the work** *which You have given Me to do.* [6] ***I have***

manifested Your name [*character*] *to the men whom You gave Me out of the world (John 17:4, 6).*

Mission #1: accomplished.

MISSION #2: Redeem Humanity

There's an old saying that to really understand someone you "must walk a mile in his shoes." This is true even in the race to save humanity: only a human can redeem a human.[1]

*¹⁷ For God did not **send His Son into the world** to condemn the world, but that the **world** through Him might be saved (John 3:17 NKJV).*

¹⁰ For the Son of Man has come to seek and to save that which was lost (Luke 19:10).

Recall that when Adam separated from God, as a new carnal being he had no power to return to God on his own; Adam could not make the good choice for God without God. Of course, that's when grace was introduced. Four thousand years later, on the cross, Jesus, the *Son of Man,* gained the victory over the Devil and the nature of sin. Jesus, the Last Adam, was able to undo what the first Adam did because He was divine in spiritual nature while housed in fallen, human flesh. With His dying breath, Jesus claimed another victory—securing salvation for man.

*³⁰ He said, **"It is finished!"** And He bowed His head and gave up His spirit (John 19:30).*

Mission #2: accomplished.

---

[1] Galatians 4:4; 2 Corinthians 5:19; Matthew 3:11.

MISSION #3: Vindicate God's Government

Jesus has declared victory in the first two phases of His mission, but there's one mission still pending. This last mission is not as obvious to most Christians: Jesus must be the omnipresent *holy Spirit* in order to vindicate God's government.

We've already learned that Jesus didn't complete everything at the cross. But we may not recognize why nearly 2,000 years later He still hasn't returned as He promised. We've had to endure another 2,000 years of sin and suffering, disasters and disease and death. Why? Because Mission #3 has not yet been accomplished.

This final phase that was initiated at Pentecost must continue until Jesus comes back. Jesus is now ministering as High Priest in our soul temple in order to be the One continual, direct, living, vital link: the one Mediator between man and God. See 1 Timothy 2:5.

[18] For through Him we both have our access in one Spirit to the Father (Ephesians 2:18).

[5] He saved us [already], not on the basis of deeds which we have done in righteousness, but according to His mercy, by the washing of regeneration and renewing by the Holy Spirit (Titus 3:5).

The reason Mission #3 is necessary is because God needs to present a convincing argument to the universe, and especially to His accusers. However, He needs more than twelve or seventy or one-hundred and twenty people. God needs a large enough community of believers to demonstrate exactly how perfectly His government functions. Jesus must prove the effectiveness and validity of God's government by actively demonstrating that it alone can produce holy, happy people, even from a fallen, carnal race. This community of believers, symbolized as the 144,000 in the book of Revelation, must consistently live out perfect faith in lockstep with Christ, under all circumstances, including under threat of death through the Mark of the Beast crisis. This is why it is crucial to understand the truth about the only two divine Beings in the universe, God the Father and His Son.

> *²⁴ Then the end will come, when he [Jesus] hands over the kingdom to God the Father after he has destroyed all dominion, authority and power [that rose up against the God of heaven]. ²⁵ **For he [Jesus] must reign until he [the Father] has put all his enemies under his [Jesus's] feet.** ²⁶ The last enemy to be destroyed is death. ²⁷ For he [the Father] "has put everything under his [Jesus's] feet." Now when it says that "everything" has been put under him [Jesus], **it is clear that this does not include God himself,** who put everything under Christ. ²⁸ When he [the Father] has done this, then **the Son himself will be made subject to him [the Father]** who put everything under him, so that God [the Father] may be all in all (1 Corinthians 15:24–28 NIV).*

> *²² who is at the right hand of God, having gone into heaven, after angels and authorities and powers had been subjected to Him (1 Peter 3:22).*

> *¹⁸ And Jesus came up and spoke to them, saying, **"All** authority has been **given** to Me in heaven and on earth (Matthew 28:18).*

As the Son of God, the Son of Man, and the holy Spirit, Jesus is God's *super Super-Champion!* No other being in the universe could qualify or accomplish this massive feat.

Jesus is still working to complete Mission #3 *in* His people—to produce a people who accurately reflect what the government of God is capable of. By understanding these things more deeply, we can cooperate with Christ in letting Him finish the work in us. Now is the time.[1]

> [1] *Therefore, since we have so great a cloud of witnesses surrounding us, let us also lay aside every encumbrance and the sin which so easily entangles us, and let us run with endurance the race that is set before us, [2] fixing our eyes on Jesus, the author and perfecter of faith, who for the joy set before Him endured the cross, despising the shame, and has sat down at the right hand of the throne of God. [3] For consider Him who has endured such hostility by sinners against Himself, so that you will not grow weary and lose heart (Hebrews 12:1–3).*

---

[1] Philippians 1:6; Daniel 12:4; Revelation 10:4; 22:10.

17

Living Like a Superhero

⁴ For the weapons of our warfare are not of the flesh, but divinely powerful for the destruction of fortresses. ⁵ We are destroying speculations and every lofty thing raised up against the knowledge of God, and we are taking every thought captive to the obedience of Christ (2 Corinthians 10:4, 5).

There are thousands of religions in the world, and each one has only self-help tips and external controls to offer their followers—except one. True Christianity is the only religion that offers a *Savior*. True Christianity is the only religion based upon the miracle of the new birth. Through the new birth, God infuses the perfected divine-human Spirit of Christ into the spirit life of the believer. By this supernatural union we inherit Jesus's experience of victory, His wisdom, His thoughts and desires, along with His character of love, joy, peace, faith etc.—fruits of the divine nature—while every thought is brought captive into obedience to His perfect will. We are adopted as sons and daughters of the Most High God in a better way than before Adam fell, for now the divine Son of God is our blood Brother!

> *16 I say then: Walk in the Spirit, and you shall not fulfill the lust of the flesh (Galatians 5:16 NKJV).*

> *6 Therefore as you have received Christ Jesus the Lord, so walk in Him (Colossians 2:6).*

Walking in Jesus is a lot easier when it's all sunshine and lollipops. Where most people fail is by not being consistent in their walk. They think it won't matter if they skip devotional time this once or pray halfheartedly because they have other things on their mind. Then "life" happens, and two weeks later they're wondering what went wrong and why they can't cope; they find prayer is now a struggle and they can't connect with the Lord as before. They conclude it must be God who has abandoned them, when they are the guilty party.

Make no mistake—we will be challenged, and often. The Devil is a sore loser. He'll pull out his biggest weapons, such as *discouragement* or *fear*. Then we're nothing more than a bull's-eye for all his "fiery darts" (Ephesians 6:16) because we've lost our Shield and everything is hitting us full force. The answer to avoid these setbacks is to be consistent and to settle in your heart to choose Christ today. Every. Day.

Trials and temptations are a normal part of life in a fallen world, but they should remind us of our utter dependence upon the Superhero for His Armor of protection and steady deliverance. Then when the going gets tough, our prayer shouldn't be to make all our problems go away. Our prayer should be for a greater revelation of Jesus in the midst of our problems, to trust Him in the moment, because we know everything is working out for our good. So, no matter how bad it seems, never give up or give in, because God will never put on us more than we can handle. We have His promise and He is faithful to keep it. [1]

> [13] *No temptation has overtaken you but such as is common to man; and God is faithful, who will not allow you to be tempted beyond what you are able, but with the temptation will provide the way of escape also, so that you will be able to endure it (1 Corinthians 10:13).*

Day by day, as our faith grows, we will start to notice how He is transforming our minds more into His likeness. Our new passion will be to seek first "the kingdom of God and His righteousness" (Matthew 6:33)—that is, *Christ in you,* and to shun anything that grieves His sweet presence. We will not only live in the Spirit but will walk in it as well. Though we may stumble a bit like toddlers in the learning process, we will continue to grow into the full stature of maturity in Jesus. We can experience all the fullness of Christ in all the power of Christ. We are not limited because He is not limited. [2]

Because we possess the One who possesses superhuman power we are equipped with superhuman power to fulfill the mission that Jesus commissioned us to do—to "go disciple all the nations" (Matthew 28:19 ABPE). This is who we are *in Christ,* and who we are cannot be altered by any outside force or circumstance.

> [3] *This is good and acceptable in the sight of God our Savior, [4] who desires all men to be saved and to come to the knowledge of the truth (1 Timothy 2:3, 4).*

---

[1] Ephesians 6:13–18; Romans 8:28.
[2] Ephesians 4:13–16.

⁹ The Lord is not slow about His promise, as some count slowness, but is patient toward you, not wishing for any to perish but for all to come to repentance (2 Peter 3:9).

Don't forget that the whole grand point of this whole grand plan is not a show of force or a strategy of war. Simply, the Sovereign God of all creation is a loving Father who has no desire to see His children lost, but wants more than anything to have us safely back home. Your Father longs for a heart relationship with you. Everything about the Plan of Salvation is about restoring you into His family.

¹ See how great a love the Father has bestowed on us, that we would be called children of God; and such we are. . . . ² Beloved, now we are children of God, and it has not appeared as yet what we will be. We know that when He appears, we will be like Him, because we will see Him just as He is (1 John 3:1, 2).

12 But as many as received Him, to them He gave the right to become children of God, even to those who believe in His name (John 1:12).

*¹⁴ For this reason I bow my knees to the Father of our Lord Jesus Christ, ¹⁵ from whom **the whole family in heaven and earth** is named (Ephesians 3:14, 15 NKJV).*

Jesus Christ really is the only honest-to-goodness Super Superhero. He has earned that rightful title because He fought the most epic of battles against the most dangerous of villains. The reality of that victory has delivered us from extinction. Today, Jesus is able to keep us from stumbling and to make us stand in His Father's presence with joy, forever!

*²⁴ Now to Him who is able to keep you from stumbling, and to make you stand in the presence of His glory, blameless with great joy, ²⁵ to **the only God** our Savior, **through** Jesus Christ our Lord, be glory, majesty, dominion, and authority before all time and now and forever. Amen (Jude 1:24, 25).*

The war is almost over and all of heaven is cheering us on to stay faithful as we near the finish line. Jesus is coming back! He absolutely is keeping His promise to take us out of this sick, dying world to be where He is! Quickly!

¹ "Do not let your heart be troubled; believe in God, believe also in Me. ² In My Father's house are many dwelling places; if it were not so, I would have told you; for I go to prepare a place for you. ³ If I go and prepare a place for you, I will come again and receive you to Myself, that where I am, there you may be also (John 14:1–3).

¹² Behold, I am coming quickly, and My reward is with Me, to render to every man according to what he has done (Revelation 22:12).

We are now equipped with this "gospel of the kingdom" message that has been restored for these perilous last days. In Christ, we have gone from the dark side of carnal flesh, as one of the living dead, to being transformed into the kingdom of light and life in Jesus. We now have our own supernatural experience and can testify to others, who are where we used to be, of the saving power of a living Savior. We can make a lasting difference in this broken world, one soul at a time. And we will vindicate God's government in the process, proving it to be the only answer for a happy universe. Our life has purpose!

²⁹ *And just as My Father has granted Me a kingdom, I grant you (Luke 22:29).*

³² *Do not be afraid, little flock, for your Father has chosen gladly to give you the kingdom (Luke 12:32).*

Wow! What a privilege to be given a kingdom! More importantly, we've been given its keys to unlock and understand its mysteries![1]

¹⁹ *"I will give you the keys of the kingdom of heaven; and whatever you bind on earth shall have been bound in heaven, and whatever you loose on earth shall have been loosed in heaven" (Matthew 16:19).*

²⁰ *And we know that the Son of God is come, and hath given us understanding so that we may know Him who is true; and we are **in** Him who is true, **in** His Son Jesus Christ. This is the true God, and eternal life (1 John 5:20).*

When we join forces with Jesus, we can live the life of a Superhero for God! This is what we were created for!

The End? It is only the beginning . . .

---

[1] Matthew 13:11.

*He has **delivered us [already!]** from the dominion of darkness and **transferred us [already!]** to the kingdom of his beloved Son (Colossians 1:13 RSV).*

*Blessed be the God and Father of our Lord Jesus Christ, who has **blessed us [already!]** with **every** spiritual blessing in the heavenly places in Christ (Ephesians 1:3).*

What's in Your Cup?

You're holding a cup of coffee when someone comes along and bumps into you, making you spill coffee on the floor, staining the carpet.

Why did you spill the coffee?

"Because someone bumped into me, of course!"

No. You spilled coffee because there was coffee in your cup. Had there been water in your cup, you would have spilled water and it wouldn't have stained the carpet.

Whatever is inside the cup is what will spill out.

Therefore, when life comes along and shakes you—which *will* happen—whatever is inside you will come out. It's easy to fake it—until you get shaken.

So, we have to ask ourselves, *"What's in my cup?"*

When life gets tough, what spills out? Love, peace, humility, patience, and gratefulness? Or is it anger, bitterness, harsh words, and bad reactions? Do you leave a stain on those around you?

If you have *coffee* in your cup you can't *choose* to spill water.

The reality is we can't choose what comes *out*. We can choose only what's inside. What's inside us is the life we possess, and what spills out is the *evidence* of that life. When our nature is carnal, what spills out is carnal: anger, bitterness, harsh reactions, self-promotion, etc.

We need Jesus in our cup. When He is what's inside, what will come out is from Him—love, joy, peace, patience, kindness, gratefulness, etc.—all the fruits of the Spirit.

Our choice is Jesus—or not. Choose Jesus!

~ Unknown, adapted

If you enjoyed this book, please leave an honest review on Amazon.

Thank you!

Transformation Ministries OTG

TransformMinOTG@yahoo.com

Made in the USA
Columbia, SC
12 December 2024

47919330R00076